My Extraordinary Journey to the

VALLEY OF JOY

By Glenda Kuhn

Table of Contents

Prologue 9
Chapter 1 Visions 13
Chapter 2 Birth pangs 21
Chapter 3 The Two Became One Family 25
Chapter 4 As the Crow Flies 39
Chapter 5 Living Can be Deadly 47
Chapter 6 Blackberries, Summers, and Ten Kids 55
Chapter 7 Pretty Shoes 63
Chapter 8 Cycles of Life 71
Chapter 9 Home Melted Away 79
Chapter 10 Continual Change 85
Chapter 11 Seek Level Paths 89
Chapter 12 Freedom Rests 95
Chapter 13 Growing Pains 99
Chapter 14 I Have Returned 105
Chapter 15 Brother John 117
Chapter 16 Tasting the Visions 129
Chapter 17 To Russia With Love 141
Chapter 18 Pilgrimage to Israel 167
Chapter 19 Hungary in November 1995 175
Chapter 20 Between the Time and Lines 179
Chapter 21 Selling Out 185
Chapter 22 Ukrainian Winters 189

Chapter 23 Bulgaria 209
Chapter 24 Meanwhile Back Home 237
Chapter 25 India 251
Chapter 26 The Nations 265
Chapter 27 Conclusion 283
Meet the Author 287
Other Books By Glenda 288

Scripture quotations taken from The Holy Bible, New International Version NIV. Copyright ©1973, 1978, 1984, 2011 by Biblica, Inc. Used by permission. All rights reserved worldwide.
Copy Write ©2021 Glenda Kuhn

All rights reserved. No part of this publication may be reproduced, distributed, or transmitted in any form or by any means, including photocopying, recording, or other electronic or mechanical methods, without the prior written permission of the publisher, except in the case of brief quotations embodied in critical reviews and certain other noncommercial uses permitted by copyright law.

Any references to historical or real events in this autobiography are the views from the author's perspective as recorded in personal journals and reflected through her experience and observations.

Formatting, Fury cover Design
Editing by Emerald Editing & Copywriting

Introduction and Dedication

"We spend our years as a tale that is told……So teach us to number our days, that we may apply our hearts unto wisdom." - Psalm of Moses 90:9 & 12, KJV

Seven is God's complete number in scripture: seven days of creation, seven days in each week, seven years of trials in the book of Revelation. Seven sevens are forty-nine then Jubilee. Throughout scripture seven is a marker for time. Some people consider it a lucky number. For me, it represents seven decades completed on the earth at the time I decided to tell my tale. Many people are involved in its telling. I cannot write about their thoughts or experiences. I can only write my own perceptions of what was happening around me and within me, the events that shaped this lump of clay into the person I became. My understanding was limited, and remains so, to the five senses: sight, sound, taste, touch, smell, plus two gifts from God, hunger and thirst for Him, seven in all, which developed during this short journey I refer to as my life.

Three streams flow through the valley where I spent my days. The gentle streams named spirit, soul, and body carried me along my earth journey. Each flowed separately, but eventually joined together to become a torrent pulling my life into a mingled current.

So many people have shared my journey that I prefer to write in generalities of events, snapshots in time, without the clutter of every minute detail.

I had wonderful parents. Each had their own journeys to follow, filled with frustration, failure, fear, laughter, learning, legacies. In their own way, they loved me. In their humanity, they tried to teach me to be an independent human being. My grandparents too, carved a road for me to follow, or not, because they also, like God, gave me free will. Their lives were my lessons, and their unconditional love was the pavement on the road of life. Just as when one stumbles they look to see if someone is watching, my stumbles in life made me wonder what my grandparents would think of me. Caring about their opinions urged me back onto the path they had carved.

My brothers and sister shared my journey from my beginning and their own. I cannot assume they knew what I was feeling, tasting, touching, smelling, or seeing. Even though we shared the same childhood road with our parents and grandparents, we were individuals, diverse ages, and developing in varied times and seasons together. We were, like humanity in general, similar, but unique.

It is my goal with this writing to help readers find pieces of their own humanity within my journey, the one which I shared with divinity and angels (spirit), teachers and mentors (soul), and other members of the species who look a lot like me (body). It is also my goal to show that including divine guidance makes me neither a saint nor a sinner, but a member of the human race who recognized a need for all three of these areas of myself to acknowledge purpose for giving more than I received during this short stay on earth.

To those in my natural and spiritual family, and to those who I have met along the way, I dedicate my story.

Valley of Joy
By Glenda Palmer Kuhn

Prologue

"For the vision is yet for an appointed time, but at the end it shall speak, and not lie: though it tarry, wait for it; because it will surely come, it will not tarry."
Habakkuk 2: 3 KJV

From the base of an archaic Communist-era monument planted firmly in the Balkans, I view red tile rooftops common to Eastern Europe. The black hard stone form of a giant man sets a constant watch over the valley from its perch on the hillside. The village of Maglish below is composed of small wood and stucco houses. Higher up the hillside is a school for children with challenges secluded in foliage nestled quietly away from major thoroughfares. My companions and a local pastor had been there to deliver adult diapers and art supplies to the students. On the way back to the Valley of the Thracian Rulers, we stopped at this monument to overlook the vastness of the lower plain toward Kazanlak.

A thousand years before I arrived here, Thracians had left their mark on the valley as they traveled through the pass, settling in its fertile soil. I knew nothing of the Thracians or the history of the small nation of Bulgaria before my journey led me from Oklahoma to this far-away place. I had seen the tombs and heard remnants of their story with each trip to Bulgaria. Thracian rulers left a rich legacy in their wake represented by items buried in their tombs, treasures of gold, weaponry used to conquer and then being conquered, of living and dying, of perseverance and hard work. Relics of their lives and how they buried their dead provided only a backward glimpse into their daily activities. Their voices were silent. Beyond the mountainside of my perch beside the monument, I let my mind muse on the twenty years I was able to leave a gentle mark on this timeless land filled with descendants of ancient humanities. The vision plays like a movie through my brain, reminding me it was not my choice to come here, but my destiny.

From the beginning of these seven decades when the valley of my life lay before me, I could not have imagined the vastness of where the inner voice was leading, nor how I almost didn't hear, or often tried to silence it.

Prologue

The following day from a mountainside near Sliven, Bulgaria, I drank deeply from artesian springs of pure water, nourishing my body and spirit. I am where the vision led.

At home, my family awaits my return.

My story may be typical of others who have been called by that deep inner voice, walking often alone in the path it leads, listening, then becoming distracted with the cares of life, aspirations of wealth, sensual desires, and being pulled again by the voice that could not be silenced.

Walking in the earth as a small woman, my footsteps were firm but quiet.

Chapter 1
Visions

"I urge, then, first of all, that petitions, prayers, intercession and thanksgiving be made for all people—for kings and all those in authority, that we may live peaceful and quiet lives in all godliness and holiness."
I Timothy 2:1, NIV

In 1984 during a break from attending Bible discipleship classes, I entered into an intense time of prayer. I experienced something that changed the direction of my life, not immediately, but like a story being foretold. The mystery of my experience unveiled as a program before a play with a cast of characters I could not have even imagined.

It was on a Monday as I cleaned my house and prayed, because I always cleaned house on Mondays as my mother taught me, when suddenly I sensed a forceful command to pray earnestly. Prostrating myself near my bedroom door, I bowed forward from my waist in what can only be explained as similar to a pregnant woman having labor pains.

Weeping for what I did not know and anguishing over what had not been revealed, a powerful force caused me to groan with waves of contraction-like physical expressions in response to a spiritual cry.

I felt as if some inner part of my being was leaving my body, but not in the sense of dying. What I began to experience in this elevated state was an image of a physical journey. As I traveled in an airplane, I looked down on the landscape below. I recognized the Eastern Seaboard of the United States, Nova Scotia, Iceland, and the British Isles from thirty-thousand feet. In my vision, or whatever was happening to me, the plane deposited me in a house in Ireland where two couples sat around a card table with their heads bowed, faces fraught by concern. I stood in a corner of the room, quietly watching and listening and praying. As I did so, one of the men looked up with a smile on his face as he shared with his friends the inspiration he received. Then, I was in the air again.

I saw Norway, Denmark, and Sweden, passing over them on the way to Russia. Curving toward the southeast, I traveled through Russia to Eastern Europe toward Turkey and Greece. I hovered, then stopped. Geographically challenged, I only knew regions, not specific countries.

From my vaulted perch, I watched a man dressed in a light-colored robe, the type worn by Eastern people, as he sat on the side of a high western-facing hillside. Even though he did not speak, I understood echoes of his heart crying for someone to show him the true God. I could not leave.

With this image in my mind, for the next three days, I spent as much time in prayer as possible while taking care of my family. So strong was the spirit of prayer upon me that I could not focus on anything during my routine other than the man crying for someone to come to introduce him to the living God.

On the third day of my unearthly experience, a woman who sometimes came to pray at my home knocked on the door. I told her I was praying and asked her to help me pray for a region that included Turkey and Greece. I explained what I was experiencing. She prayed with me and agreed with me for the people of those lands. Shortly after she left, I was suddenly lifted eastward from the region of Turkey and Greece, touching down to make a quick stop in India. Then the vision ended.

Like a prelude to a beautiful symphony, I sensed something more than a vision coming. I related it to being similar to the beginning of a song I imagined the shepherds heard at the birth of the Messiah, rolling from hill to valley, echoing throughout the remainder of my life, constantly calling me to pray for the people in the countries of my flight.

My conclusion on this experience was it was God's invitation to be an intercessor, engage in prayer for those who did not know how or could not pray for themselves. I committed my heart to keep these countries over which I had soared in the vision as a constant part of my prayer life.

*****

Before this vision, I had an encounter with the voice of God through which I understood He would plant my life in my hometown, McLoud, Oklahoma.

Dreams are the opiate of youth. As young married people with young sons, Donnie and I dreamed of going to Alaska. He planned to work as a fireman and I as a licensed nurse. We saw the ads recruiting people with our skills to join the Alaskan pipeline construction. We heard amazing stories of those who stepped into the waters to join the pipeline communities in the vast northern wilderness. Donnie and I discussed whether to sell our home or rent it out while we were gone. I could almost smell the pine and feel the cold Canadian air when I daydreamed of making the big adventurous move. Our sons would love it!

As we considered options, I went to church early one evening to practice piano and worship alone. The Spirit spoke to my heart, "Unless a corn of wheat falls into the ground and dies, it cannot bring forth fruit" (John 12:23 KJV).

I refused to acknowledge what the Spirit said to me through this verse. I ignored the all-familiar inner voice because I knew God was asking me to die to my own desires and allow myself to be planted by Him. I knew intuitively it would not be Alaska. I murmured, "I don't know what you mean."

Instead of rebuking the lie, the Spirit repeated the message.

I stopped my fingers from scaling the keyboard, looked up into the white, popcorn plaster covered sheetrock ceiling and told the Lord if He wanted me to stay in McLoud, to live and die there, He'd need to bury me because I was unable to bury myself. I wanted to go to Alaska.

With my final submission to the voice, I made one request, "I ask You one thing, Lord: That You allow the seed of my life to go around the world."

A few weeks later, I continued praying at the altar bench after church service was dismissed. The congregation left except for a few who visited with each other near the back door. I lingered in prayer.

Suddenly, it seemed as if I were being transported. The Spirit took me throughout the town of McLoud, showing me every house and allowing me to pray for the families behind each door. The Spirit took me to one street I did not recognize in the small town I lived throughout most of my life.

On the way home from the little Assembly of God Church, I turned from the main highway and found the street I did not know was there. This confirmed that the vision was of God and not my own imagination. I sensed God would open every home in McLoud to me. When? How? I did not think about it. It was God's plan, not mine. My own will craved Alaska. I did not tell Donnie about my experience at church. Instead, I ask him if he still wanted to go to Alaska. He admitted he did not believe it would be a good decision. We did not discuss the move again.

In scripture, forty is the number for testing. Forty days in the ark for Noah. Forty years in the wilderness for the children of Israel and forty days and nights for Jesus Christ in the wilderness before He began His earthly ministry.

Every event in my life, the joy of early childhood, the pains of growing up, failures and small successes had led me to this place where my spiritual ears were open. This open heart had required nearly forty-years.

Chapter 2
Birth pangs

"There is a time for everything, and a season for every activity under the heavens." Ecclesiastes 3:1 NIV

I was born just after midnight on the first day of winter, 1948, a bitterly cold morning on the cusp of Sagittarius and Capricorn. Of course, I do not remember the event. My mother told me Dad drove the old car slowly to the Okemah hospital from Paden because U.S. Route 62 was icy slick. She said it was cold for a few weeks, so cold that snow, like fine talcum powder, dusted through the leaky ill-fitting windows in the old house where she, my Dad, and my brother lived. My great-grandmother owned the old, dilapidated house. My mother later told me she snuggled in bed all day with my brother while Dad was working because there was no wood to heat the house. Mostly they survived on cornbread and milk, and lots of pinto beans, but it kept them from starving. She told me the beans sometimes included a little pork when Dad made enough to buy some or if her Papa gave them some.

In case you have never heard of Paden, Oklahoma, it was, at the time of my birth by longitude and latitude, the most prolific site for tornadoes in the United States. It was pretty much dead center of Oklahoma Territory when it was settled in the late 1800s. My great-grandfather, my mother's paternal grandfather, moved his family from Kentucky to Keokuk Falls, Indian Territory, a small settlement on the North Canadian River southwest of Paden. That would make me the fourth generation to live in Central Oklahoma.

The delivery room was wicked cold, Mama said. Her contractions were coming fast, too fast. Suddenly, the doctor commanded she stop pushing.

"The cord is around the neck!" he shouted.

Without the assistance of a nurse, he moved quickly to retrieve an instrument, rushing back to the immediate task of unwinding the cord from my neck. I was already turning blue and Mama wasn't able to quit pushing with the next contraction. I slipped from her womb. Catching me, the doctor turned me like a corkscrew unraveling the umbilical cord. Using a rubber suction bulb, he pulled mucus from my mouth, then slapped me on the backside. Mama said I screamed right away, but it took a lot of crying for me to pink up. The doctor wrapped me in a blanket, laid me on Mama's stomach, and scolded her for having another child so soon after her first.

My older brother George William, named for his grandfathers, Charlie George Davis and William Andrew Bird Palmer, had been born eighteen months earlier on September 8, 1947.

My parents named me after a foster child who was placed in the home of my Dad's sister, Violet, and her husband Elmer. While they were trying to adopt Joyce, she was placed in another home, leaving them devastated. Because I was born just before Christmas, Mama changed Joyce to Joy for the season. Glenda is the feminine of Glen, a small valley. My name in meaning became Valley of Joy. Aunt Violet and Uncle Elmer later divorced. A namesake was no substitute for an empty womb.

Dad was a Texan and wanted Mama to convert, but jobs were more scarce in Red River County, Texas, in the late 40s than they were in Oklahoma, so the tug of where to live began. They moved to Texas where Dad found day jobs in sawmills, worked with the Bruce and Son's Moving Company, hired out as a ranch hand and horse tamer, and anything else he could find. Mama and Dad both chopped cotton or pulled bolls, depending on the season, to bring in a few more dollars. Then they would see greener financial grass north of the Red River only to move back to Texas when Dad became homesick. Finally, they moved into the first house I remember. It was down the lane from my maternal grandparents.

My mother's name was Sylvia, which means "out of the woods." It seemed fitting that she always loved being outdoors, but heartbreaking because her responsibilities kept her inside. While living in the house behind her parents, Mama gave birth to two more children: Kathy Lorene, when I was three, and Billy Bruce seventeen months later. Kathy's middle name was also Mama's middle name. Bruce was named for Dad and the West Texas moving company family name, Bruce and Sons. My parents would have a third son, James Stephen, four years after Bruce.

My childhood would not be guided by visions or dreams, but by the discipline and guidance my parents and grandparents gave me.

Chapter 3
The Two Became One Family

"Therefore shall a man leave his father and his mother, and shall cleave unto his wife: and they shall be one flesh." Genesis 2:24, KJV

Dad, Billy Joe Palmer, joined the Marine Corps near the end of World War II while living near Bagwell, Texas. Before he saw combat, he was discharged because the war had ended. He and my mother, Sylvia Lorene Davis, met in 1946 on a train heading eastward from San Diego, California. She was returning to Oklahoma after working in a cannery on the west coast. Joining their lives in marriage in November that same year, blended the Palmer and Davis families into one, a group I knew as *my* family.

Grandparents on both sides of the border were loving and attentive, but not indulgent. I watched them put in gardens, draw water from open wells, make lye soap, quilt from scraps, repair motors, and generally make do with what they had in their non-materialistic environment. I loved to hear their stories, especially those about children.

*****

Palmer Branch in Texas

My parents and brother left me with my paternal Grandma while they went to the cotton field. I wanted to go too, but Mama said I was too little. I cried. Grandma Palmer held me and they disappeared out the front door. It is one of my earliest memories. There would be too many more to record.

"This one?" I asked Grandma Palmer over and over as we picked string beans from Granddad's northeast Texas garden. The bean plants were bright green and grew shoulder high on my two-and-a-half-year-old body. If Grandma nodded affirmatively, I would pull with both hands until the bean broke away from the plant. If she said, "Not yet," I left it. When she said there was enough, we both went inside to break and string them. The beans and potatoes with a little fatback added for flavor would be served to the family, along with cornbread and polk greens, when they returned from the cotton patch.

Dad and Mama usually took us to Texas for Christmas. Grandma Palmer always made a two-egg cake with a cup of black walnuts to add flavor. Granddad used a vice to crack those black rock-hard nuts, but I sure was glad he was willing to do it. Grandma would bake the cake in her wood stove and slather it with her home-made muscadine jelly or some of her jujube jam.

Every Sunday Grandad Palmer loaded up any grandchildren staying in his house and drove them to the Bagwell First Baptist Church. Sitting beside him on a pew, watching him pay attention to the sermon, bow his head in prayer, and sing from the hymnal made me wish I knew how he met God and they got to know each other so well. Grandma Palmer did not go to church. When I asked her why she did not go to church, she told me she would have to wear shoes if she went to church and she did not like to wear shoes. I had looked at her earthy stained bare flat feet as she sat in a rocking chair near the fireplace, spitting snuff juice into the flames. Perhaps, I concluded, she did not own a pair of shoes except the cloth ones I saw her wear when she cooked breakfast on cold mornings.

My paternal grandparents, William Andrew Bird Palmer and LuElla (Tidwell) Palmer had eleven children, seven survived to adulthood, four boys and three girls. They provided a trove of grandchildren.

I was curious about my grandparents' lives but enjoyed little individual time with them. One afternoon my opportunity came to have that one-on-one with Grandma Palmer. She told me about her four children who had died. Each had been born healthy, like the other seven. But each died unexpectedly, one of a spider bite, another from pneumonia, another from complications of childhood disease, and another from circumstances Grandma held inside her heart. Grandma Palmer told me the stories of her lost children over and over because I asked about them over and over, any time I could carve out a little time alone with her. So concerned about these lost babies, I committed their names to memory, so they would be remembered as having lived and were loved. Their names were recorded in a family Bible, Charles Ervin Palmer, Dec. 22, 1917-June 20, 1919; James Cleveland Palmer, November 24, 1922-May 15, 1925; Ruby Christine Palmer, November 22, 1925-December 6, 1925; Margie Ruth Palmer, February 5, 1929-December 1, 1929. Hearing her stories made me wonder how it would have changed the family had they survived, or my family if I had not.

These stories made me want to be what they could have been. I know that may sound unusual for a young child to sense something so deeply. It was a connection I could not quite make at the time, but was acutely aware of it.

When we lived in Oklahoma, Dad always seemed a little sad and busy working. But, when we visited his family in Texas, he laughed and had fun. We had fun too, free to run and wander around my grandparents' forty acres without much supervision. Family was a community for the Palmers. It was one unit of many parts. Not everything worked perfectly. Actually, there were numerous imperfections, bickering and heated discussions. Yet, if anyone ever came to visit, they were family and could become partaker of those discussions. Everyone was welcome at the table or to use a bed or to come any time.

For the most part, we ate biscuits and gravy for breakfast with eggs if the hens were laying. In the center of the homemade table cushioned with a printed oilcloth, was an island of bottles and jars, clear and dark Karo syrups, sorghum molasses, salt, pepper, toothpicks, and sugar. On special occasions, we had chocolate gravy. I believed chocolate gravy was the Palmer secret dish. Mama learned to make it, since she had become one of Dad's family.

Mama told me Grandma Palmer had unusual cures for just about any ailment. Grandma was a little superstitious, too. She did not like the number thirteen or black cats. Grandma believed tobacco could be used for much more than snuff or rolling up in white cigarette papers for smoking. A big swallow of tobacco eliminated intestinal worms, according to Grandma. But Mama wouldn't try it because it was tobacco and she thought God didn't like tobacco. Grandma also used tobacco to make a poultice to draw infection from a sore or spider bite. My cousins who lived just up the road from Grandma and Granddad told me Grandma saved snake skins and kept them hung in Granddad's wood shed for wound care. She would cover the wound in sugar and kerosine and put the snake-skin directly over the wound to hold it all in place. My cousins said it worked, so their mother used the poultice too.

During one visit to East Texas, Mama learned my cousins had chickenpox. Grandma Palmer had a preventative measure. She shut her chickens up in the coop and told Mama to tell George and me to lie down across the gate. Then she shooed the chickens right over us. Even though Mama did not believe in the cures and she hated tobacco, she told me later that George and I had only a couple of chickenpox sores after the chickens flew over us. My cousins were subjected to this treatment too. They had lots of sores, but none ever had a scar from the pox. Mama seemed to be convinced that *something* helped us stay chickenpox-free. I could see my northern Mama was learning some things from my southern Grandma.

On her left arm, Grandma Palmer had "blackberries,"' which is what she called the bulging purple raised patches on the upside of her left elbow. When I asked her why those purple lumps were on her arm, she proudly told me they were her "blackberries." Every year when blackberries were ripe, little seeds would come up, she said. Sure enough, I saw it with my own eyes the very next spring. Seeds popped up all over those raised purple spots making those lumps look just like blackberries. Grandma said her mother must have picked blackberries when she was pregnant with her. It happens, Grandma declared to me, so every woman should be careful about where she goes and what she sees early in pregnancy or the baby could be "marked." Grandma Palmer knew a lot about surviving.

Davis Branch in Oklahoma

Before I went to school, life was filled with fireflies, June bugs, and watermelon seeds that grew through your ears if you swallowed them, or so I was told by a stranger who was plowing my maternal grandfather C. George Davis' field. My brother and I liked to play beneath a small clump of trees on the south side of the house. He and I constructed a table using discarded tin cans and an old board we found. I learned to make the best mud pies of anyone I knew. Of course, I only knew my brother and parents, grandparents, and a few cousins. My mud pies were the best. I know it because everyone who saw them always smiled when I showed them how deftly I decorated my pies with green grass and dandelion puffs.

The Davis family went to church a lot, usually twice a week, three times if you counted Saturday nights. Services at the Paden Free Holiness Church actually began Saturday night at seven o'clock and ended whenever worshippers quit singing, often around midnight. If I was sleepy during service, I would lie beneath a pew and sleep until time to go home. Grandma Davis said Saturday night services were held because Saturday nights were the devil's night and going to a church service kept those who attended out of the devil's reach.

Every meal began with a prayer of thanksgiving. Mama called this prayer "returning thanks." I cannot remember the first time I heard The Lord's Prayer or the 23rd Psalm or John 3:16. "Amazing Grace," "The Old Rugged Cross," and "I'll Fly Away" were tunes of daily life, and I cannot count the times I heard Grandpa Davis lead a march around the altar bench singing, "When the Saints Go Marching In."

Dying was not something I thought about at all until Mama shared the story of her brother. Mama said she was the largest baby born alive in Okfuskee County, Oklahoma, in 1927, weighing over fourteen pounds. Her older brother weighed more, but he had not survived. Eight children of Charlie George and Julia Emaline Davis did survive, three boys and five girls who gave their parents many grandchildren. My mother was the fourth child, or fifth if you count Baby Boy Davis, the one who died.

I always liked to listen in on my parents' and grandparents' conversations. Mama said I should not eavesdrop, but she let me stay around when she and her sisters talked about their husbands, recipes, new household gadgets, and having babies. I knew if I was quiet and still, they would ignore me and I could stay nearby and listen. Instinctively, I understood the subjects being discussed were for sisters only, not to be shared outside the group.

Talk of the Great Depression, post-war challenges, and the scars left from 'the service' seemed to be daily conversational fodder in each branch of my family, but especially the Davis branch. My maternal grandfather, Charlie George Davis, served in World War I. Two Davis sons, George and Cleo, went to World War II, both wounded in action. Both survived, Mama said, because of the prayers of her mother. I had heard my Pentecostal grandmother pray, and sing and wave her hanky in the air at church service as if she was chasing the devil away. I believed with certainty her prayers were the reason her sons had survived, and the extra Saturday night services surely helped keep the devil out of Grandma's mind so she could trust God that her sons would return.

Grandma Davis planted a garden every year. She always wore a bonnet, a long-sleeved dress, and most often an apron. Mama said the garden was where Grandma went to pray. When I asked what praying was, Mama explained it was just talking to God. I instinctively knew Grandma Davis was not to be interrupted when she was praying, so I just watched her from the kitchen window. I wanted to know what she prayed about and if God ever answered. I wanted to ask Grandma how she knew God heard her and how she knew to pray for her sons when they were in the war, but I did not ask.

Every time I saw Grandpa Davis (Papa to his children and some grandchildren) outdoors, I would beg to go with him. He was always doing something interesting such as trading for a goat or a horse or some piece of machinery. He would show it to us, or let us ride the pony or play with the goat. In a few days or weeks, whatever he had bought, animal or mechanical, would be traded for something else or sold. He bought (or traded for) a wringer washing machine for Grandma. It was quickly enlisted as a toy, especially when the cousins came to visit. All that playing with the washing machine stopped after my cousin's arm was pulled between the wringers. It was a lesson on the difference between a tool and a toy.

Mama's youngest two sisters were still living at home, when we lived nearby. Clarice liked to come visit and carry us around. Zelma was younger and liked to read a lot and visit with friends. They were both at church, though, even on Saturday nights. Mama's brothers were married and lived near enough to stop by their parents' house regularly, so they were always at church too, except Cleo. He and his wife, Jane, went to the Baptist church. The whole group of Davis siblings liked to gather together to make home-made ice cream and let the children play.

Members of Mama's family helped each other if needed, but the goal, Mama explained, was to seek independence so it was not necessary to ask for help. She said I should be independent when I was eighteen, but the age of accountability would happen when I was about twelve or thirteen years old. Mama said once a girl knows right from wrong, she is responsible to God for her actions. I counted how many years lay ahead to reach those markers in my journey and filed it away for future reference.

Permanently Home in Oklahoma

The Red River battle ended permanently the year Dad was hired at Tinker Air Force Base. The drive to work was long from Prague, but permanent income established a sort of permanent residence north of the Red. The winter I turned five, Dad and Mama moved away from my Davis

My Extraordinary Journey To The Valley Of Joy

grandparents to a small house just north of Harrah, Oklahoma. We stayed there long enough for George to be enrolled in second grade and me in first. Even though my birthday was in December, Harrah Schools allowed me to start. Mid-term, my parents moved four miles north of McLoud, Oklahoma. McLoud Schools told my parents if I continued the second semester there, they would have to pay for kindergarten. So, I was a first-grade drop-out of sorts, since my parents did not have money like the rich folks Mama sometimes talked about.

That was the first time I understood the concept of rich and poor. If a family was rich, they could have and do much more than those who had little.

My Dad's oldest brother, R.H., initials for Robert Henry, also moved his family to McLoud and camped out in an open rock structure across the intersection from where we lived. He was a World War II veteran and also had been hired for a job at Tinker Air Force Base. His children were about the same age as us, so we were delighted to have a Texas family in Oklahoma.

My mother's sister, Marie, was a business teacher at McLoud High School, which may be why Dad and Mama moved there. Aunt Marie and Uncle Bill were rich because they owned a camera that made movies, real movies. Their house held everything a girl my age could want. She and Uncle Bill lived in a new house and owned a beautiful car. They even had air conditioning in both. Their indoor toilet was decorated with a fuzzy rug in pink, my favorite color, with a toilet topper to match. My parents took us there to visit on the Fourth of July. We sat in the backyard and watched fireworks. I had never seen anything so beautiful or heard anything so loud. Aunt Marie said the fireworks launched at the end of the McLoud Blackberry Festival. I was sure Grandma Palmer's blackberry birthmark was seeded at that time too.

Chapter 4
As the Crow Flies

"The rich and poor meet together; the LORD is the maker of them all." Proverbs 22:2 KJV

A whole new electronic era opened up to the Palmer kids in the rented house four miles north of McLoud. We became rich because Dad bought us a television. The eye to the world occupied the southwest corner of the southwest room of the four-room house. A pot-bellied wood stove occupied the opposite corner in winter. Suddenly, we were no longer limited to weekend television with Aunt Marie and Uncle Bill. We could watch our very own television even on Saturday nights because the church in McLoud did not have Saturday night services. Images of a larger expansive world came to us, powered by a single wall plug, all with the turn of a knob.

The first winter we lived there, Dad and I trudged through the snow to a dilapidated barn just south of the house to bring back unpainted boards to fuel the stove. The kitchen also served as the place where Mama filled the galvanized tub for us to bathe. We pumped the water from a hand pump outside the back door and heated it on the propane kitchen stove. We lived in a two-bedroom house, but Dad and Mama let us three oldest sleep outdoors in the summer on a mattress topped metal frame bed settled just below an open window. Baby Bruce slept in his little bed just inside the screen.

That summer Grandpa Davis brought us an injured crow. Mama wrapped its broken leg with a strip of rag. Grandpa said we could teach it to talk while its leg healed. The crow let us pet it and ate from our hands. It seemed to like us a lot. George, Kathy, and I talked to the crow so much, we were almost hoarse from repeating words. Despite our efforts, one day it just flew away without ever talking. Sometimes best efforts are not immediately rewarded.

My parents bought me a doll for Christmas the year we lived in the house north of McLoud. I named her Mary Lou. My cousin Renda, who lived in the rock building nearby, received a similar-sized doll that same Christmas. She named her doll Betty Sue. From then on, Mary Lou was always with me, always.

I felt so happy as a first-grade dropout because Renda and I started first grade together. That year youthful, beautiful Phyllis Foster taught her first class at McLoud. She played the piano as the class sang together. I liked watching her fingers glide across the keyboard. Watching her play made me want to play piano someday.

At recess, Renda and I would swing and pretend there were alligators beneath us trying to reach our feet. A red-haired boy named Cecil sat near me in first grade. He was my first crush because he was kind and handed me a pencil when I dropped mine. I understood kindness.

In 1956, a person could buy a loaf of bread for a quarter and have a little change. McLoud first-grade students went on a year-end field trip. It cost each of us ten cents. Mama gave me a quarter to pay for the trip, buy a treat for myself and bring a nickel home. After we returned from the trip, I wrapped my nickel safely in the corner of my handkerchief. Before class loaded onto the afternoon bus, Mrs. Foster told us a story about a fellow student with no food in his house. The teacher suggested we ask our parents for a little money to bring to school the next day to help the family. Someone in the class had money and gave it immediately. I untied the nickel from my handkerchief and gave it to Mrs. Foster for the family.

When I arrived home, Mama asked me about the nickel. I said I did not have it because I gave it to a needy family. She scolded me, which felt like an unmerited emotional spanking. I did not cry, but I learned giving away what you have been entrusted to keep is wrong, even if it is for a good reason. Mama knew some lessons were best learned through quick targeted pain so they would not be forgotten and that life lessons were best learned young.

Mama still wanted a house of her own. She persuaded Dad to go look at a house west of McLoud. They bought it along with fifteen acres of land. An old house doesn't necessarily mean a dilapidated house, but in this case, it meant well-used and in desperate need of repairs. The house came with a dirt dugout cellar beneath the kitchen, which Mama called a root cellar. I didn't worry much about tornadoes, but I sure was frightened to go into that cellar.

The rough old house offered one convenience I loved, a modern bathroom with a real bathtub. No more outhouses! No more baths in the kitchen! Being rich felt really nice. The enamel-coated cast iron bathtub served its intended purpose and a number of other purposes, including keeping a big bucket for crawdads seined from our shallow pond. As Mama canned, the bathtub made a great reservoir for George, Kathy and me to wash canning jars. Bruce was not old enough to handle glass jars when we first moved in, but he would get his taste of the kids' work, hoeing a garden, washing canning jars, peeling fruit, feeding chickens, milking, and helping Dad work on cars.

A partitioned portion of the bathroom became my brothers' bunk bed space. Mama finally bought her first electric washing machine and the bathroom also became the washroom with a drain hose pulled out the bunk side back window. After all the clothes were hung outside on Monday, Mama would drain the washer and mop the bathroom real good with her rag mop. I used a discarded toothbrush to scour away buildup on the floor around the pedestal sink and commode screws. Mama said that's the only way to get things really clean.

There was an enclosed porch off the kitchen which was delegated as a sleeping space for Kathy and me. In the winter, Mama used the space as a second refrigerator because it was so cold. She stored late summer fruit, pears, and apples, under our bed because they kept so well in the cool room. In the summer, the heat drove us to open windows and doors to beg for a summer breeze, or to sleep outside.

Mama got busy with her sewing machine, the one she bought just before we became rich. Using printed feed sacks, she made curtains for the open shelves in the kitchen. Black iron kettle images on the feed sack fabric provided a contrast to the red florals popping out of the kettle lid. Mama loved red more than any other color. Long springs were pulled through a small hem on top of the curtains. A small bent nail on the cabinets held each end of the springs. If the curtain was pulled too firmly when putting up dishes, the spring provided flexibility. The hem allowed Mama to pull the curtains back while she put up dishes. Mama was smart like that, always thinking about the best way to make things pretty. The kitchen bloomed, thriving with smells of food and a continual orchestra background of children's voices. Our wooden kitchen table also served as a game board and a place to play jacks. The old house became a home.

Just after we moved into the house in late 1956, Mama said she was pregnant. I remember being excited about my new brother or sister. Mama taught a Sunday School class at the McLoud Pentecostal Holiness Church where we attended services. One Sunday as she taught about the first Christian martyr, Stephen (she pronounced it Stefan), she said she decided she might name her new baby Stephen if it was a boy. On May 1, 1957, James Stephen Palmer was born.

My maternal grandmother came to help care for the baby and us because Mama returned to the hospital with blood clots in her right leg. She experienced the same problem after Bruce was born, but the clots dissolved. This time she would return to the hospital shortly after bringing the baby home and endure vein stripping to prevent further clots. I never knew why Grandma Davis left our house, but I know she left without saying goodbye to me, which made me sad. After Grandma Davis left, Dad called me, all of eight years old, into the bedroom where my baby brother lay on my parents' bed. "Sis, you are going to have to take care of this baby."

Responsibility was not short-term. Taking care of James Stephen was a lifelong commitment in my eight-year-old mind, but I would learn responsibilities can be delegated and life can be short.

Chapter 5
Living Can be Deadly

"A happy heart makes the face cheerful, but heartache crushes the spirit." Proverbs 15:13 NIV

Death changes people. It changes them inside in unreachable places. Death alters families and relationships inside the unit. Like a pebble thrown into the water, each action by a human being has a ripple effect. Joy has the same ripple effect, but joy comes in short supply after death slams so hard it warps the family circle. With experience, I understood how the effects of death linger, often generationally.

Starting third grade meant learning cursive, a craft I found fun and worked very hard to master. I squeezed the pencil so hard, it scarred me for life, a large bump on the index side of my middle right finger. Another scar shaped our family that year, a deeper eternal oozing cancer from which it never recovered. It was a dress rehearsal for the upcoming main events in the lives of the children of Billy Joe and Sylvia Lorene Palmer.

In December 1957, Mama picked me up from school because my dad's brother, Harvey, died in a construction accident. Uncle Harvey left behind a wife and five daughters. Just two years older than Dad, Harvey was his best friend and childhood comrade. Something died in Dad that day too. Something irreparable happened so deep inside him he could not fully express it, so it oozed slowly throughout his entire consciousness.

The broken branch of grief seemed to bounce onto other branches, cracking them, then knocking them to the ground. Like dominoes stacked on ends, a cascade of deaths in my Dad's family began, one toppling right after the other. With each funeral, another notch etched itself in an ever-deepening chasm in Dad's soul. The cancer of grief spread to every area of his life.

After Uncle Harvey's death, his family moved from a ranch in West Texas to an old house near my paternal grandparents just north of Bagwell. One pleasant side effect of their move from West to East Texas was our ability to visit them more than when Uncle Harvey worked on a ranch or in construction. I liked that my cousins were closer because Eula Mae was just older than me and Barbara just younger—instant playmates when we visited our Texas grandparents.

The next summer, I spent two weeks with my Texas grandparents and my cousins. Mama warned me two weeks was a long time, but I wanted to go. Granddad and Grandma Palmer lived in a house north of Bagwell, Texas, at the end of a long lane hidden from the main road by pine, walnut, oak and bois d'arc trees. A house near them had become a home for Uncle Harvey's grieving family.

Like a cluster of Little Red Riding Hoods, during my two-week visit, my cousins and I walked through the piney woods to visit Grandma's friend, Mrs. Taylor. We teased our grandmother and irritated our Granddad, enjoying every minute of time with them. We made chocolate gravy for a late breakfast. We huddled like puppies beneath Grandma's or Aunt Vida's patchwork quilts each night telling silly, scary stories and giggling at our own jokes.

That summer, my Dad's youngest brother, Jessie, brought his sixteen-year-old wife to meet his parents. My new Aunt Virgie became instant friends with Uncle Harvey's oldest daughter, Mary. They took us to my first drive-in theater in Clarksville. I had never seen a movie before because Grandma Davis always said if Jesus came back and I was at a picture show, He might not find me there. I don't remember what we watched, just that I sure was glad Jesus waited for me to leave the drive-in.

Granddad was never really clean-shaven, except for church. On summer days he often sat on the porch with his two or three-day-old facial growth dressed in khakis and a sleeveless undershirt. To me, he must have a shadow of whiskers to look natural.

One Sunday morning during my stay, I lay on the living room bed and watched him shave. Lying on my stomach with chin propped in both hands, I looked up to see his reflection in a broken piece of mirror held to the wall with two twisted nails. A small shelf beneath the mirror held his shaving mug and brush. A razor strop hung beside the shelf. He brushed on the shaving soap with a short little fluffy brush, then rubbed his straight razor across the strop. He tugged the razor over his left cheek first, then his right, then under his nose and on his neck. I couldn't figure out how he could shave without cutting himself. When I grew old enough to shave my legs with a Gillette, I bounced the sharp-edged razor up the front of my leg leaving telltale pockmarks that didn't heal for weeks. I thought of Granddad, still fascinated by his precise use of the sharp razor.

During my two-week Texas stay, I watched my grandparents in their home and talked to them individually. Grandma told me the story about her lost babies for the last time that summer, perhaps because she lost another, Harvey, seven months before.

I had never been away from home for so long, so by the time Granddad and Grandma Palmer took me home to Oklahoma in Uncle Harvey's blue car, I felt really homesick.

When we arrived home, there was a sense that I had returned to routine. I was happy to be home in Mama's kitchen with the cheery curtains. But, I would be forever grateful for that sunlit summer because of the unimaginable dark cloud slowly edging toward our family.

In December 1958, I turned ten. Mama always made a cake for supper to celebrate our special day. Sometimes Mama gave us a little token gift, but not always. I never expected a gift. I also didn't expect my tenth birthday to be the beginning of the end of my childhood.

Near the end of the 1958-59 school term, the class took a trip to visit a nearby newspaper office. We saw the layout room where the staff used tilted, standup desks for paste-up of the preprinted newspapers. Near the end of the field trip, the newspaper tour guide showed us the press room. It smelled of ink, oil, and old papers. The smell lingered in my nostrils even after we boarded the school bus, a smell I never forgot. The odors were ones I longed to inhale again.

The McLoud Monitor listed the death of my paternal great-grandmother, the second Palmer family domino to fall, in January 1959. Three weeks later we gathered again to bid farewell to her youngest son, Johnny Andrew "Dyke" Tidwell, only forty-six years old. In July, a third domino fell with a resounding thud: Granddad died. I could not believe it. He was fine when I saw him at Granny's funeral and at Uncle Dyke's funeral. Mama said Granddad (William Andrew Bird Palmer) died suddenly that summer while watching a movie at the Lamar Theater in Paris, Texas. I knew it wasn't true.

When we attended Granddad's funeral, I could not believe everyone actually thought he lay in the casket. It was a trick, I felt sure. As I stood alone in the parking lot after services, I concluded Mama was wrong this time, and if she was wrong, so was everyone else. I had seen the body lying in the casket with my own eyes. Granddad Palmer always wore khakis and glasses. The man in the casket wore a suit and no glasses. He was clean-shaven too. Everyone was mistaken, except me.

A recurring dream haunted me, a dream of denial in which Granddad moved far away with another family, but became homesick to see me and returned. Dreams, regardless of how real they seem, often fade with time.

Dad never recovered from one stroke of death until the next one hit. Uncle Harvey's accidental death plummeted him into a deep depression. He wanted to take care of Uncle Harvey's five daughters, but we lived in Oklahoma and the family chose to stay in Texas. Losing his adored grandmother thirteen months after his brother was like plunging a dagger deeper into an already open wound. Death's ripple became a tsunami, breaching secure foundations in the

Palmer family on both sides of the Red River, and extending to generations not yet born.

Death marks an end or a challenging new beginning.

Chapter 6
Blackberries, Summers, and Ten Kids

"Children are a heritage from the LORD, offspring a reward from him." Psalm 127:3 NIV

Everyone who lived in or around McLoud, Oklahoma joined the effort to keep blackberries flowing from the fields to market. My brothers, George and Bruce, sister Kathy and I picked blackberries every summer. After Uncle Harvey died, his daughters visited us during blackberry picking season and joined us in the fields. These were real blackberries on a bush, with thorns, not like the ones on Grandma Palmer's arm. Blackberries were the cash crop in McLoud then, hailed as the Blackberry Capital of the World with more blackberries raised, picked, packed, and shipped from McLoud, Oklahoma, than anywhere else in the world. We took pride in knowing we lived in such a famous town.

Beginning in June, a black truck rumbled past our house early in the morning, on its way to the Chambless blackberry farm less than a half-mile west of Mama's house.

Men, women, and children headed for the berry fields filled the back of the black flatbed truck with wooden sideboards. We got up early in the morning while it was still cool outside, ate breakfast, put on our long-sleeved shirts and a hat, and picked berries until lunch. We primarily picked blackberries on the Chambless farm, but over the years of living in and around McLoud, we would experience many blackberry bosses and a slight increase in wages. None, however, were as familiar and kind as Johnie Chambless.

Long after we returned home for beans, cornbread, and sweet iced tea, I climbed into an elm tree and watched the old black truck driving men, women, and children back home. It made me happy we lived close enough to quit picking berries about noon.

When my brothers, sister, cousins, and I made enough money at three cents a quart for picking blackberries, Dad, Mama, and Aunt Vida took us to Springlake Amusement Park in Oklahoma City and to the Oklahoma City Zoo. Like the blackberry field workers, we piled into the back of Dad's pickup truck and made a day of spending our hard-earned cash.

It occurred to me many years later that Mama and Aunt Vida took care of ten children in that house with the real bathtub and too-hot bedroom because that's just the way things were. We ate a lot of beans, cornbread, and fried potatoes, and we always owned a cow for milk. Mama splurged occasionally and made a chocolate cake that she would poke holes into and then pour homemade, hot fudge into those holes. When Uncle R.H. (Dad's eldest brother) and his wife Aunt Ruby came out to play dominoes, there were fourteen children playing Red Light, Green Light, hide-and-seek, Mother May I?, and Simon Says until Mama made us come in and the company went home.

An empty pasture west of the house made a great sandlot for baseball. Relatives from both branches of my family came on Sunday, played baseball games and everyone participated. Dad skipped rope with us. If it was raining, we played jacks or hide the thimble in the house. Mama and Aunt Vida laughed as they worked and then laughed about the mishaps of the day. They never seemed to run out of things to say to each other. Summers were full, but like the lives who lived them, were all too short.

Mama divided household chores among the girls and outside chores among the boys. It always seemed to me there were a lot more inside chores than outside. Since

Mama made the assignments, I think she just knew more inside jobs that needed to be done.

I helped Mama hang out laundry every Monday, her washing day. Before she bought the washer, and again after it broke, she always went to Underwood's Help Yourself Laundry in McLoud. I liked going there because I could watch James, and he and I could play in the open troughs of water that swooshed by when the washers emptied. Mama took the wet clothes home in a big wicker basket to be hung to dry. Even in winter, we pinned some on the clothesline and hung rags and older clothes across the barbed wire fence between the yard and pasture. When the temperature fell below freezing, the clothes became stiff. Mama said they freeze-dried. When the clothes dried, we brought them inside through the cheery kitchen and folded them on Dad and Mama's bed then each of us put away our own clothes. I always kind of liked wash day.

Mama decided she needed to earn a little extra money so she sold Avon products while George, Kathy, Bruce and I were at school and my baby brother James was old enough to leave with a sitter. Mama traded our neighbor Mrs. Blake babysitting for Avon products, a barter that gave each of them something they wanted. Occasionally after school let out, Mama allowed me to go with her on deliveries. Through these calls, I became acquainted with some of the Kickapoo women north of McLoud. They were good Avon customers and seemed to appreciate Mama including them in her route.

On one sales trip, we visited a Kickapoo family with a summer house in the backyard. Many Kickapoo families constructed a traditional structure of raw wood and branches with leaves. It was cooler for sleeping during the summer heat. The customer noticed my curiosity, so she asked if I would like to see it. The warmth inside the house cloaked me with a sense of security, and I made a spiritually deeper, unexplainable ancestral connection in that summer house. Mama said she saw a snake the size of a stovepipe on the way to the Kickapoo lady's house, but I wasn't afraid. Something about the calmness of the house and the hospitality of this friend, made me feel safe, even from stovepipe-sized snakes.

Grandma Palmer had always been afraid of coming north of the Red River. She said her mother was also afraid of crossing the Red. After Granddad died, she evidently completely overcame her fear of being north of the Red

River. When she came for a visit Mama used sweet-smelling Avon talcum to sprinkle on Grandma's feed sack dresses and muslin slip when she ironed them. Grandma seemed to appreciate Mama's effort. She sniffed the ironed dresses and muslin slips before she pulled them over her head, smiled widely, then straightened them like a queen would her royal robe. Their relationship blossomed.

When Grandma Palmer stayed at our house, she brought squares of fabric to sew together for quilt tops. She taught me to cut quilt squares using scrap newspaper for backing to prevent the small pieces from stretching. She lit a creative torch in me when she helped me sew my first nine-patch.

One day, Mama came home from her Avon route after trading ten dollars in Avon products for a piano. The old upright required a lot of space in our small house. Dad, who strummed guitar and blew a harmonica, plucked out tunes on the keyboard.

He taught himself the guitar and liked to turn the television to Country Music shows Saturday nights. Dad's family told us when he was a teenager in East Texas, he and his brothers, Harvey and R.H., hitchhiked to Nashville to audition for the Grand Ole Opry. In the tryout trio, Dad played guitar, Uncle Harvey yodeled and Uncle R.H. played the harmonica. They didn't make it to the big leagues, but it wasn't for lack of confidence and hard tries.

Mama always said we should try anything, at least once. She mostly said this about food, but she did not allow us to use the words, "I can't," about anything she told us to do. If we slipped and said those words, she said, "Can't never could do nothing without they tried."

I think Dad heard the words Mama said too. He tried and tried to play that piano.

Chapter 7
Pretty Shoes

"You did not choose me, but I chose you and appointed you so that you might go and bear fruit - fruit that will last." John 15:16 NIV

A pair of pretty shoes can make a girl feel like a woman. Sensing a metamorphosis, I could only think of one accessory to help me feel more mature, pretty shoes. Mama decided I was no longer a child. After Granny died and Uncle Dyke died and Granddad *may* have died, I asked her for a pair of pretty shoes instead of saddle oxfords. She told me I was old enough to start earning money to buy my own extra things, so if I wanted pretty shoes, I needed to get a job and buy them myself.

I set out to find myself a job. Renda's mother, Aunt Ruby, worked at a small café about a mile-and-a-half from our house where I was hired to bus tables on Saturday mornings. I made enough in about three months to buy myself a cute pair of white flats with pointed toes. I bought white because Mama said white went with just about everything. My saddle oxfords dried out for lack of polish and wear. I never wore another pair of saddle oxfords.

Like Dorothy of the Wizard of Oz, something about those shoes elevated my self-image. I knew I had somewhere to go in addition to Mama's house.

I began hearing God's voice inside my heart. He didn't speak in a thunderous mountaintop experience, through a phenomenal miracle, or like an old man in the sky through a hail storm and wind, or tragedy. God spoke to me in a way a child hears, softly and tenderly, yet authoritatively. He spoke through a heart-to-heart encounter within the environment I lived with family and friends as I took daily steps in my journey through life.

During the summer, I took off a weekend from the cafe and stayed for two weeks with my cousin. Her parents, my mother's eldest brother George and his wife Pearly Jane had six children and owned a dairy farm. On their farm north of Paden, I learned to get up early to milk cows and help use and clean a cream separator. I developed a taste for a tablespoon of sweet rich cream on my morning cereal, which made it melt in my mouth like a sweet pastry. I tasted green apples picked from trees, but learned there were consequences for eating too many.

From my cousin's family, I learned people do not need pretty drinking glasses for good-tasting iced tea. It was just as sweet and cold when drunk from a plain, clean tin can. Their lives were like the tea in the cans and the cream on my cereal, served simply but rich with potential.

Uncle George and his family attended church Saturday nights, Wednesday nights, and twice on Sunday at Burnett Mission north of Paden, so I took my new shoes along to wear to church. Otherwise, we went barefoot.

At the end of a Saturday night service in the old white church building located on the corner -- the one with the homemade slat benches, the rough altar bench, and single bulb lights -- the preacher asked if anyone wanted to get saved, to repent of their sins and give their lives to Jesus Christ. Music played. Women sang. Men prayed. The congregation waited. I knew I needed to move forward and give my life to Jesus. My Sunday school teacher in McLoud taught me that everyone needed to move forward. But I didn't really understand why I needed saving and what I needed saving from. I knew the urge was real, coming from outside my mind deep inside my person.

As the young girl played the old upright piano and more women sang, I gripped the pew tightly. The fear of stepping into the unknown was greater than the fear of holding my place there behind the pew. The Spirit of God urged me, calling me for His purpose, that much I did comprehend. Something in the pit of my chest, just beneath the breastbone seemed to ache. I didn't feel guilt, but a sense that some wrong needed to be righted deep inside my being.

Relief washed over me when the service ended, and happiness filled my heart when my parents came to get me the next day. I never went back to spend two weeks with Uncle George and Aunt Jane again, not because of the experience in church, but because life around me changed.

A few months after church with my cousin, I stayed with Mama's sister, Clarice. She took her children to every church service every week of every month. Yes, Aunt Clarice went to church more than anyone I knew. And she prayed a lot at home, saying phrases like, "Praise the Lord," even when she sighed. She let me stay up after she put her young sons to bed and drink Dr Pepper, Double Cola or root beer floats with her and Uncle Roy. One time she let me drink strawberry soda with vanilla ice cream, which was heaven to my taste buds.

She took me to the library near their house. Aunt Clarice read quickly. She read the books she checked out and then read the ones I checked out. Then, we took them back to the library and checked out more until I needed to go home.

On Sunday evening, Aunt Clarice, her little boys, and I walked together across her back yard to attend services at a small Assembly of God Church. I noticed a handsome young man a few years older than me playing the drums. I always dreamed of writing, so I looked for characters for my stories or rhythm for my poems. This young drummer looked a lot like I imagined one of the characters in a historical novel. Settling into the familiar rhythm of church service, singing along with the songs I learned by rote, stealing glances at the drummer, I feared he might look back.

The preacher preached, but his sermon seemed hollow. I only remember him asking if anyone wanted to give their hearts to Jesus. I did want that, but I was afraid it meant giving up myself. I wanted to give my life to Jesus Christ so very much, but I did not want the drummer to think I was dirty or marred in some way -- a sinner. I desired to give my life to God so badly I felt I would die if I did not go forward.

I gripped the pew in front of me and held it tightly. Like the cord around a child's neck during birth, something prevented me from opening my inner being and inhaling the Spirit. Something needed to turn me like a corkscrew to unwrap me so I could breathe, but what? More miserable than before, I left the church, appreciative of the darkness shrouding us as we walked home. I wept as I lay in the darkness on my temporary living room couch bed and wiped my tears on the pillow because I feared God might not offer me another opportunity to accept Him.

My experiences in church services taught me I needed to perform a sequence of activities to be 'saved': go to the front of the church, let people see me cry, and be assured by the pastor of my acceptance. But, I argued in my head, it wasn't the pastor's voice I heard. In the darkness of the living room, I begged God to give me another chance so I could give my life to Him.

I feared God didn't really want me, a dramatic dreamer who became angry when someone picked on her friends. A vain girl who liked picture shows and perfume and pretty shoes.

A Sunday school teacher said Jesus loved me, but God hated liars and I lied. I stole sweets from the refrigerator, even when Mama said we could not eat any leftover chocolate gravy or a spoon of molasses.

Grandma Davis said God wanted me to have long hair and wear clothes that covered my arms and legs, and I could never wear makeup, or be beautiful because that was vain, and Mama cut my hair and kept telling me I could be more beautiful if I tried. Then silence consumed my heart.

Chapter 8
Cycles of Life

"Flesh gives birth to flesh, but the Spirit gives birth to spirit." John 3:6 NIV

The first Oklahoma summer of the 1960s my parents took my younger siblings to an evening Bible school at the Pentecostal Holiness Church in McLoud, where Mama always took us to Sunday school. Sometimes we stayed for church service, but usually, we just went to Sunday school, then Mama went home and cooked a big Sunday dinner.

I did not want to go to the Bible school. But, when my parents let my younger siblings out of the car, my old Sunday school teacher with the long, blond, braided hair twisted in a ring on her head, wearing long sleeves and a high collar, peeked through the passenger window and begged me to stay. Because I loved her and saw her sincerity, I agreed to stay for Bible school, but in my heart, I intended to make it only one night then hide from Sister Phillips the next night. After all, *Bible school was for little kids.* I sat on the back row of the church, where I could daydream to satisfy my boredom and keep the voice beneath my breastbone quiet.

The first night, a missionary named Sarah Honeywell gave a flannel graph lesson on the beginning of sin in the earth. She had long hair, wore plain clothes. There was not a hint of makeup on her face. She was a missionary to the Navajo Nation in Arizona and during summer breaks went to small churches hosting Bible schools, which was the most interesting fact I learned from her. Why she chose McLoud to host a Bible school, I did not know. Her niece Joyce, played the accordion for the music portion. Sarah urged us to sing to the accompaniment.

A budding people-pleaser, I wanted my former Sunday school teacher to see my sincerity about church, so I decided to continue to go every night. I didn't really have anything else to do, and I liked to watch Joyce play the accordion. I was fascinated by the fact that the keyboard on the accordion was the same as a piano. I began to save my blackberry picking and babysitting money to buy an accordion.

Each subsequent night of the evening Bible school, Sister Honeywell continued her theme of explaining sin's origin, God's dealing with it, and finally introducing the One who could remove its damning nature, Jesus Christ. Through her explanations, I began to understand with my mind what my heart heard and what the voice inside me invited me to do. The sin nature was born of my imperfect human parents, both of them, and my grandparents from ancient generations to the beginning of time as humans know it.

The only way to remove that nature was to take on a new nature, an eternal living spiritual nature, only available through the One who transcended death, Jesus Christ. I deserved death because of my sin, but Jesus offered His blood to cleanse me from it. Somehow it made sense that God could create a new spirit, even for a flawed girl. Forgiveness for all my separation from my Creator seemed like something attainable. Finally, I had understanding that joined me with the voice in my heart.

Sister Honeywell gave the invitation, and I remembered my promise to God while lying in the dark on Aunt Clarice's couch: if given another chance, I would give my life to Jesus Christ. I cannot answer for others, but for me, this was now or never. I was convinced of it in that place just beneath my breastbone deep inside. I couldn't move from where I stood, even with the pressure in my heart that felt like a volcanic fire trying to force its way out. No preacher stood to shake my hand or accept me. Everyone else seemed to disappear. Even though people stood all around me, the experience was an intimate, just a God and me session. I knelt at the prayer bench (altar) and wept bitterly. I wept for what the Son of God had done for me. I wept because I disobeyed his voice but He invited me for a third time anyway. I wept with a sense of grief, knowing from that moment on, I was no longer myself. I became another person inside. I did not know the fullness of this transformation, but I knew I had forever changed. Like a washed cat, I felt clean and confused.

What I experienced went against all I knew, but it was more splendid than I imagined inner cleanliness to be. I was absolutely happy and euphoric at the sensation of my new birth. I could breathe again. At that moment I understood the *why* questions in the meaning of divine appointment. Sister Sarah Honeywell came to McLoud to explain to me the why of needing Jesus Christ, the answer I needed so I could step into a new inner life.

Then, Mama arrived to pick us up from Bible school.

The younger children rode home in the back seat. I rode in front with Mama. Just as the car passed the McLoud Riverside Cemetery on the way to our house, I shyly told Mama I got saved. She said that was good, but offered no other comment. I wanted to dance and run and for her to sense the joy I had because of what happened to me. But, it seemed, she did not understand that I'd changed, that something fearful and wonderful had happened inside me.

Outwardly, I am sure Mama could not see any difference, but I knew I was different. Later, I understood the child I was had died and some new force resided in my spirit. Unlike my natural birth, Mama and Dad had nothing to do with this. I became a participant in another place, another realm. At the moment I announced to Mama my new personal relationship with God through Jesus Christ, I sensed an independence from her while at the same time feeling a responsibility to her as if she were one in a world filled with people with whom I was connected. I was different and the way I interpreted our relationship in view of this new one forever changed in an instant of saying yes to the voice.

The preacher said I needed to be baptized in water to show I had died to sin and been raised to eternal life. Without a baptismal at the church, the pastor baptized me in a small muddy pool secluded from Harrah-Newalla Road by scrubby blackjack oak trees.

Just as my toes reached the dirty pond water, someone whispered, "I saw a snake over there by the bank."

I closed my eyes and pushed my right foot into the water. It touched oozy earth. My weight pressed goo through my toes. My left foot followed. Both feet were engulfed by what I could not see beneath the dirty liquid. A woman's fear-laden whispering about snakes played a mysterious melody in my brain. I challenged the dirge with thoughts that if God could save my soul, His Holy Spirit could very well protect my body during baptism.

My hand-me-down cotton dress floated up around me like a raised sail. I wondered whether I showed some indecent portion of myself, but, one glance at the dirty water convinced me no human eye could see beneath the thick, brown-gray, gravy liquid from which frogs jumped onto a grass patch.

Pastor Koehn smiled and reached for my hand. I smiled back and stepped forward. The muddy ooze covered my ankles and sucked my feet deeper. Each step toward the outreached hand became an effort to free first one foot, then another.

Our hands touched. He guided me closer. I could smell his aftershave. He covered my mouth with a dry, white handkerchief and said, "I baptize you in the name of the Father, the Son, and the Holy Spirit."

He pushed my body backward. My heart raced. I held my breath. I closed my eyes tighter.

When the preacher lifted me up, it was done and I was sealed, my commitment complete. I heard clapping from the banks. I hoped they were happy and not shooing away another snake. For a moment, fear of the slithering varmints shot through my brain before I pulled loose my foot from the pond and stepped out onto the dry bank. The sun beamed down. I felt safe and secure while sensing an ancient attachment, similar to the Kickapoo summer house experience.

Those gathered kept singing the same stanza of "Shall We Gather at the River." I thought a different song would have been more appropriate. A river would have been far better and much cleaner than the old pond. I searched the banks to see if I could glimpse a snake, but saw nothing but dragonflies, a swarm of gnats, and a few frogs jumping around on the opposite side. I pulled an old towel Mama brought over my head to cover my long, mud-caked hair.

The baptism sealing my eternity seemed an ominous forecast of immediate life. We did not notice then, but many challenges slithered into our lives, striking with venom.

Chapter 9
Home Melted Away

"I have seen the burden God has laid on the human race. He has made everything beautiful in its time. He has set eternity in the human heart; yet no one can fathom what God has done from beginning to end."
Ecclesiastes 3: 10-11 NIV

Dad wanted to sell Mama's house, the only one we lived in long enough to call a real home. The house held memories of cousins and sleepovers and sibling rivalry and sandlot baseball. Yet Dad struggled every day. His memories churned of family losses, haunting his nights. He wanted to quit Tinker Air Force Base and move to be near those who remained of his family and the graves of the dead. He ached inside and out, and no one could reach the root of cause.

Dad began losing weight. Never a heavy man, the pounds were significant. He complained that his heart and stomach hurt. His posture became stooped. His lips turned downward. A local doctor diagnosed him with ulcers and instructed him to drink lots of milk, which seemed to make him more ill, so he continued to drink his strong coffee instead. He hated his unchallenging job at Tinker. He disliked hauling trash for people in McLoud and dumping it in the ravine on the acreage, a service he provided to make extra money. With a long, drawn-out sigh, he said he needed to relax to find peace. Peace only comes from the absence of struggle. Dad continued to struggle in his mind, body, and heart.

Dad laid aside enough garbage-hauling money to build a garage. Mama said Dad never finished anything, though. She pointed to the large trash and water-filled hole in our backyard he dug for a real cellar but never completed.

Uncle R.H., his older sons, Marion and Ronnie and my brother George, along with some neighbors helped Dad put up the frame of the garage, nail the sides, even partition off a room in the back where Dad set up a cot so he could get away and rest. He put on a roof, but like Mama noted many times, he never completely finished the garage. The incomplete garage became a retreat from his job, an unhappy wife, a lot of active children, and memories of loss. He sequestered himself by working on cars, tinkering with tools, and sipping on wine to help him relax.

Never one to be silent on anything, Mama told me she worried about Dad's drinking. She suggested we children break his jugs of wine, telling us where he kept them in his garage behind the partition near the cot.

We took no pleasure in breaking Dad's bottles, but Mama continued to send us to break them, the big wine jugs, and later the gin, and then rum. Dad never punished us for doing it. He simply bought more with money that should have been used for better food for the family.

One day Mama said I couldn't go see Uncle R.H. and Aunt Ruby anymore because they were divorcing. Uncle R.H., and his sons, Marion and Ronnie, started coming to our house often to eat beans and cornbread and Mama's chocolate cake. But Renda and her younger brother, Benny, moved away with their mother. Finally, the judge gave Uncle R.H. full custody of his four children. They stayed in their house in McLoud one more summer.

Then with one decision, a dagger split my security apart. Dad's only relative north of the Red River moved south after resigning his position at Tinker and took away my best friend and cousin Renda.

Mama started crying a lot then too. School was out. Grass, mingled with young sand burr sprouts, pushed through the soil on our baseball field. We never played anymore, anyway.

One Sunday we didn't go to Sunday school. Mama always took us to Sunday school, so I felt a little lost. I didn't know how to fill a Sunday morning without church. Mama peeled tomatoes and cried, so I asked her what was the matter. She said she wanted to go to church, but couldn't because she had too much work to do. She didn't want my help with the tomatoes, so I left her alone to process what was out of her control and beyond my comprehension.

What better sense of freedom for a young girl than a set of wheels. A neighbor gave me a bike. I learned to ride it by coasting down the hill in front of our house, so I went out to practice my new skill. Once I learned to balance and stay out of the ruts on the dirt road, I was on my way to freedom. I practiced on the rutted road all morning before I felt confident enough to experiment with riding the bike in the yard. I peddled up the driveway, past Dad's garage, made a long turn by the fence, and I was knocked off my bike by an unseen metal wire to the neck. Landing on my back, I raised my head enough to see the bike crash near the door to the dirt cellar beneath the house. I saw and pedaled around an old stump where Dad cut down a tree. What I did not see was Mama's newly strung clothesline wire between Dad's garage and the out-building where Mama peeled the tomatoes for canning. Unseen unexpected obstacles have a way of knocking a person down on a long downhill coast.

Mama began telling my brothers and sister I was Dad's favorite child. Dad never said it and her saying it made me think she and my siblings would be happier if I went away. I had learned the story of Joseph in Sunday school, how he was sold by his siblings because his father loved him more. I became afraid of my family's rejection. I began to entertain the idea that my family would be happier if I were not part of it. Mama often urged me to go stay with friends from school or with my cousins.

Dad's drinking escalated. He drank wine and rum and gin, really any type of alcohol. He missed too much work by calling in sick or using vacation time. Mama and Dad fought often. The only relatives who came to visit us then were Uncle Roy and Aunt Clarice on Sunday afternoons to play dominoes. They let me play when someone needed a break, but I developed a disdain for competition. Mostly, I liked to practice playing Jacks where there was no competition except against my own skill because competition meant someone lost. It always made me sad to know someone else had to lose for me to win.

One Sunday, no visitors came. After lunch, Dad and Mama took their usual Sunday afternoon rest nap while we watched television or played games. Mama came out of the bedroom. She pulled me into the kitchen away from the others. Mama asked me if Dad ever sexually abused me or touched me in private places on my body. I told her he had not, but she had already accused him. He would never hug me or sing to me or tickle me or call me sweetheart again, ever.

I did not play much forty-two dominoes after that night. I quit playing Jacks. Grass and sand burrs grew another season over the bases in the ball field. Although I am sure there were some happy times in my life afterward, I do not remember laughing, truly laughing from a deep place of carefree joy. I eventually forgot how to play.

Dad and Mama sold the old house. With their signatures, our home vanished. Daddy left Tinker on medical retirement for a nervous condition. It was the beginning of many moves we would make, all within the community of McLoud. Each move was a new start that never led to a better family path.

Chapter 10
Continual Change

"Make it your ambition to lead a quiet life, to mind your own business and to work with your hands, just as we told you, so that your daily life may win the respect of outsides and so that you will not be dependent on anybody."
I Thessalonians 4:11-12

Dad was never lazy. His medical retirement check from Tinker did not cover the basic needs of a growing family, so he worked various jobs. I can't remember a time when he didn't hold a job. He was willing to work, diligent to be on time, and happy to put in a full shift.

Mama went to work too at the McLoud Public Schools lunchroom where she earned a regular paycheck and shared a schedule with her children. I saw the lunchroom from my first-grade class when I began school in McLoud in 1955. I coasted on roller skates from my classroom to the lunchroom many times. The McLoud lunchroom was a little bit of home. In that building, Mama learned how to make big batches of menu items to feed school children, including fluffy hot rolls, my personal favorite. While she worked there, she downsized a recipe for Wacky Cake, a recipe without eggs or oil. That cake became a family favorite.

Mama said since I did not have a job, I needed to work at the cafeteria before school to earn my own lunch. No pay didn't sound like a good job to me, but if it helped Dad and Mama make ends meet, I was willing. I could set the tables for the elementary children, she said. A few weeks later, Mama told me I could also work my lunch break. I wiped away uneaten food before putting dishes in the automatic industrial dishwasher, which paid for one of my siblings' lunch. Mama always found a way to make do. Then, she told me since I was not allowed to wear shorts or jeans for physical education because of the holiness dress codes of the church, I should work in the lunchroom during that class to pay for another lunch.

When James Stephen started first grade, I picked up a second shift during lunch. I wasn't alone. Some of my best friends at school also worked in the cafeteria to earn their lunch money. The next school session, I was not given the physical education class shift, so my sister Kathy worked lunch breaks too. George also swept and mopped the lunchroom in exchange for his lunch. Bruce never worked at the lunchroom because of after-school practices, but he ran a paper route. Every member of the family contributed where they could to help Dad and Mama provide for all.

Mama brought school cafeteria leftovers home, so our family often ate the same meal for supper that we enjoyed a little fresher at noon. Weekend meals were special though. Saturdays we made bologna sandwiches for lunch and sometimes we had a hamburger for supper. George worked at Bird's Store in McLoud where he bought a pound of hamburger meat, which Mama mixed with an oatmeal extender so it fed the family. He also bought RC Cola and peppermint candy to share. On Sunday, Mama put on a roast or chicken before church. She usually made a dessert on Sunday too.

One winter while Mama worked at the school lunchroom and Dad worked as a plumber's helper, Dad's niece and her family joined us living in our rented two-bedroom house near the school. His niece was pregnant with her third child. Because the baby might need a blood transfusion at birth, doctors wanted them near Children's Hospital in Oklahoma City. While they lived with us, Dad's sister and her two youngest children also came to stay a few weeks until the baby was born. During the Christmas season, a nephew came from Fort Sill to see his sister and mother, and younger siblings. Fifteen people lived in our concrete block two-bedroom house across the street from the school lunchroom. Dad was happy. He was working. His niece's husband worked with him. Dad had members of the Palmer family living north of the Red. His drinking diminished for a while. I did not hear Mama complain about the crowds, either.

The Pentecostal Holiness Church brought a big box of food for Christmas, but Dad said he did not want charity. Even without charity, that was the best Christmas since the year in Mama's house when she cut a dead tree branch, glued bits of cotton on it, and planted it in a coffee can for a Christmas tree. It occurred to me then, Christmas was not defined by having many things, or even a big fancy tree, but by being surrounded by many people who deeply cared about each other: family.

After Dad's niece had her baby and all the relatives went back to Texas, we moved again. Our parents rented a house with three acres of land and a large garden spot.

Dad changed employment. He was drinking again.

Chapter 11
Seek Level Paths

"Make level paths for your feet and take only ways that are firm. Do not swerve to the right or the left; keep your foot from evil." Proverbs 4: 26-27 NIV

Time seemed to be moving more quickly. Life took on the series of highs and lows typical of a developing teen-age girl. I sensed my days flowing like a roller coaster with disorganized moments of elations and devastations. Just when I thought going up would last forever, a new direction -- a different rental house, a new friend at school or church -- caused the upward swing to drop into an even deeper and faster slide. The only solid part of my life at that point became my Bible and the church.

A baby cries when it lacks the language to express its pain or desires. Writing poetry, like a baby's undeveloped sound specific language, continued to provide an avenue of expression through which I could release my anger and frustrations. Occasionally, I wrote of beauty, usually centered on biblical principles of hope, amid the darkness encroaching on our family.

Conventional wisdom says Mark Twain quipped, "It is not the things I do not understand about the Bible that trouble me, but the things I do understand that scare me to death." I do not know if he really said that, but I understood the churning in his heart, a cry to understand, aligned with the fear of understanding things beyond the natural realm. Yet I was drawn to understand the Bible by the inner voice that constantly bubbled up when I wrote dark poetry exuding its light into the struggle.

I tried to talk to Mama about praying and my faith, but she just kept telling me I was becoming fanatical. The more I ingested God's Word with its simple life principles and promises, the more my hunger increased for understanding some of the experiences I was having in prayer. People's faces flashed through my mind when I knelt beside my bed or went into the closet to pray. No preacher or Sunday school teacher or my praying Grandma Davis said anything about what I experienced. Some faces I recognized; others I did not. The Apostle Paul wrote that believers should pray without ceasing. I did not fully understand Paul's process. Despite my lack of understanding, I wanted to be obedient to pray for those I saw. Since Mama did not understand what was happening to me, I asked the pastor's wife what the Apostle Paul meant about praying without ceasing. She told me Paul's statement did not mean I should stay on my knees all day, but she never explained what it did mean. I realized she did not know, nor had she experienced the concept.

Three elderly ladies from church lived in the heart of McLoud. Sometimes I stopped by one of their houses on the way home from school or Sunday afternoons before church because they were always home and always enjoyed my visits. They listened to what I said. We talked just for the pleasure it brought to each of us. Sister James, Sister Phillips (Markham), and Sister Rooms talked to me about their younger years. We conversed about their children and grandchildren as we proudly looked at family photos. They also shared adventure stories from their childhoods. I enjoyed hearing about their simple lives growing up on farms. I was reminded of my uncles and grandparents as they told me heartbreaking events of sending husbands and sons to fight foreign wars.

While poor, even by my family's standards, the women were rich in knowledge and understanding of life. Personal history and spiritual context made sense when I listened to them. Christianity for them was a lifestyle. They didn't just go to church and pray but lived every moment in the understanding of a relationship with God who lived inside anyone who offered themselves as a tabernacle. I learned from these older friends that life on earth was not easy or forever, but God's principles stood eternally. They understood my prayer experiences and shared with me their own stories of triumph and failure.

One year, missionaries to Brazil came asking for donations for their service in South America. Russell West, his wife, and three young sons fearlessly chose to plant their lives in a nation of people who spoke a different language, living far from extended family and the United States. I found myself fascinated by their passion to leave everything to dedicate themselves to others.

Perhaps I could be a missionary to Mexico.

Mexico was closer to home than Brazil, I concluded from the pull-down map on the school wall, so I could still come home in case my brothers or sister needed my help or Mama needed help with Dad.

The next summer when the West family came back to the States to raise support, Russell died when his car ran off the road near the Arbuckle Mountains. His wife returned to

Brazil with their three young sons to continue the work alone. I pondered their situation often, her courage to follow the course with her three young sons, and I contemplated if my dedication would have been as strong. I wanted it to be stronger.

When I was about fourteen I started playing the piano at church. Mama had sacrificed a year of weekly lessons for me to learn before she could no longer afford it. But, I could read the top note on a hymn and improvise with the left hand. Mama always made sure the old upright piano came with us to every rental we moved into. We had moved five times in as many years.

Dad still longed for Texas, for family, for peace, but there was limited family still in Texas and peace has to come from within, not with outward circumstances. I could tell he was thinking just like me, how he wanted things to go back the way they were before Uncle Harvey died, before Granddad died, before the wine, before he got sick, when we had fun in the sandlot near Mama's house.

When Dad and Mama fought, or Dad didn't come home, I wrote more poetry. Putting my thoughts and feelings on paper seemed to ease something inside me. Like the psalmist, I used this poetic outlet to praise, weep, express despair and hope, even to get angry. If ink could scream, the world would have heard my voice, perhaps from an upper window at Griffin Memorial Hospital where Dad was temporarily sent and where Mama would threaten to send me if I did not stop praying, fasting, and hiding in my room to write.

Chapter 12
Freedom Rests On Responsibility

"If you hold to my teaching, you are really my disciples. Then you will know the truth, and the truth will set you free." Jesus Christ John 8:31-32 NIV

Our family moved to 8th Street in McLoud into a two-bedroom house with a garage. The door of the garage seemed small when I hit it a few times trying to pull into it with our 1955 station wagon. I learned to drive in that standard shift two-toned green albatross. If I could drive it with my head held high, I could not be vain about my personal image.

Dad's drinking was escalating then. His youngest brother, Jessie Lee Palmer, worked at Tinker and moved to McLoud just across the street from us. In earlier years, having family close helped Dad, but it did not have the same positive effect this time. He was becoming increasingly moody and worked sporadically.

Mama did something amazing. She bought the house next door. Mama was satisfied, except for Dad's drinking. I had found contentment too.

The mid-60s began a decade of freedom. Because Mrs. Ferrell, my Home Economics teacher, was persnickety about matching seams in sewing class, she helped mature the sewing skills I learned through 4-H Club. With the money I earned from little jobs, I bought fabric, patterns, and thread to sew my own clothes. Shift dresses were in style and easy to make.

Velma Prince, who worked dry goods at Bird's store, helped me choose fabrics. She assisted me with colors and patterns and trims to enhance them. My self-image came into better focus. For me, it meant exchanging my "holiness" clothes for the homemade stylish shift dresses, a shroud of frivolity in uncertain days. For the first time, I looked closely in the full-length mirror and liked what I saw staring back at me. I still did not wear slacks or jeans or shorts, just dresses, like the preachers instructed. But, at least I could create fashionable ones on Mama's sewing machine.

Long hair was proper for a good Pentecostal Holiness girl, but I wanted to find a style for my heart-shaped face that would be more attractive than braids or buns the older women at church wore. I looked longingly at the highly-teased, short hairdos worn by many of my classmates. I thought the style would cap off my new look nicely. But I kept my hair longer because the preacher said godly women wore their hair long. In my desire for acceptance by my peers, I rolled my hair on orange juice cans, as I heard upper classmates say they did to get volume, and teased and sprayed it for stability. I cut thick shaggy bangs that would have impressed any Beatles fan. The thick brown fringe hovered just above my wing-tipped glasses. I wasn't the best dressed in McLoud, but I believed I could at least walk with my head held high.

I felt free for the first time since I was ten. I laughed a little, especially when a small group of friends or cousins and I were allowed to stay out later on Friday and Saturday nights when we could cruise between the Linda Jane and Sonic drive-ins in Shawnee looking for cute guys and perusing the newest "look."

Yes, Dad continued to drink, but his addiction developed a rhythm. When he came home, Mama told me to take care of him. I told him I loved him, which made him cry. I led him to the bedroom, took off his shoes and pulled a blanket over him and he slept.

When he called from jail, Mama loaded us up to get him out. When we got home she told me to take care of him. I told him I loved him and he cried. I led him to the bedroom, took off his shoes and pulled a blanket over him and he slept. I experienced days off from the routine… the days he did not come home at all.

Chapter 13
Growing Pains

"You will hear of wars and rumors of wars, but see to it you are not alarmed." Matthew 24:6 NIV

Young men were drafted for the military and sent to Vietnam. I hated the war. The Cold War earlier in the decade was a "what if" war, left to our imaginations and playing on our fears. Vietnam was a real-time war. Some of my cousins were drafted or joined up and served a tour in a country hard to find on the world map. Upperclassmen from McLoud High School were drafted and sent, returning home drastically changed as if their life had somehow been sucked away from their bodies. I had three brothers. Who could predict how long the war would last?

Dad bought me a 1956 copper and cream Chevrolet Bel Air with glass pack mufflers. I had not asked him for a car. Mama said I didn't deserve it. I didn't. She deserved and needed a car because she was financially supporting the household. I was expected to pay Dad back with my after-school and before-school jobs. I worked for a family five mornings a week getting their children off to school and walking them home. I also sat with children on weekends. My budget could handle the car payments as long as the job lasted and I could stay at home.

I was almost seventeen when Dad bought the car, nearing the age Mama said I should be independent. According to Mama, I needed a better job since I owned a car.

When school was out my junior year, she took me to Midwest City, where she pulled her car into a restaurant parking lot and waited while I applied for a waitress position. The meanest man I ever met hired me. I hated the job. I hated the city. But Mama said she only made enough money each month to feed herself, my sister, and two younger brothers, so I must move out when I turned eighteen or start paying rent for living in her house. My oldest brother George had heard the same message from Mama the year before and moved to an apartment in Shawnee. I needed money.

To understand why Mama would force her daughter to help support the family financially at such a young age, it is necessary to know it was something she drew from her own experiences.

Mama grew up during the economic despair of what is often called The Great Depression. During her childhood, a nickel could provide food for several hungry mouths. It took a lot of work to earn a nickel then. Food, whether fruit, vegetables or meat, was raised by the family or neighbors. Flour, sugar and many other things were rationed. Families were held together with the glue of co-dependency.

As the eldest capable daughter, Mama was her mother's helper in all things domestic. During World War II she worked summers to help the family sustain itself. She became a Rosie-the-Riveter of food processing when she went to California to work in the food supply chain. She postponed her senior year in high school to continue to work in California canneries. When the war ended, she came home to graduate at Paden High School a year late, then went back to California the next summer.

By the time I was a teenager, she had been through a different kind of war. After Dad began to drink heavily, she fought for her dream of having 'good kids'. She watched as other branches of the Davis family prospered financially, while her resources dwindled from an uncorked bottle. She had lost a few battles - her first home, her security, her self-worth. Once she found emotional independence from Dad's addiction, she needed George and me to contribute to fill the financial holes in the family budget that included five children, four of them teenagers.

I was weary too. I had become self-centered, goal oriented to fulfill my own dreams instead putting what I perceived as her problem to bed every night. My contributions obviously would not be enough to fill the void in her marriage. So I chose to marry on my eighteenth birthday to a strong protective older man who I convinced myself would help me reach my goals.

Loneliness crept in like fog, eventually obliterating all personal hopes and dreams. My faith was shrouded by a blanket of self-condemnation. As a police officer, his companionship was with his brothers in blue and his family of which I felt like a teenage dangling appendage. I did not fit anywhere. The fog lifted momentarily every-other-weekend when his children came to visit or we took them to his parents' home in Tahlequah.

During our marriage, all money I earned was deposited into a checking account that did not include my name. We changed addresses five times in seven years with only his name on the titles. I had found better jobs along the journey.

Going from waitress, to secretary, to finally a warehouseman at Tinker Air Force Base. Each of these provided some sense of value that I was earning my own way in life. My foggy fiscal status became a continuation of what had been before I married, making a contribution without acknowledging personal goals.

Meanwhile, Mama was rebuilding her new life. She divorced Dad shortly after I married. She remarried in 1970 to Johnie Chambless, the bachelor blackberry farmer we picked for growing up. Johnie was a kind, loving husband, a good example of manhood to my sister and younger brothers who still lived at home. He must have been picked by God for Mama because he became the best grandfather the next generation could have. He loved family. He enjoyed fishing. He taught each of us the application of impartial unselfish love through his willingness to give himself fully to the healing of the family he invited into his home. It was comforting to know my brothers and sister lived in a calm environment and someone watched out for them.

I enjoyed going to Mama's home again for Sunday dinners and fellowship with my siblings.

Nineteen months after Mama married on the event of my fifth wedding anniversary and my twenty-third birthday a ray of hope appeared amid the day-to-day heaviness. The addition on that day persuaded me that despite my absolute failures, God still heard my prayers and read the letters I had written to Him on lonely evenings. As if to confirm He was still with me, through a series of miraculous events, God gave me my own son.

Chapter 14
I Have Returned

"Come, let us return to the LORD." Hosea 6:1 NIV

I was home in McLoud again.

One night, at the youth pastor's invitation, I spoke to twenty students at the youth group.

How many times had I attended that little church? The church and I shared a history, a lifetime of Sunday mornings, Sunday nights, and Wednesday nights together. It is where I played the piano and cried over my sins and spent many hours trying to understand the dress codes. That church was where my dreams of becoming a missionary were birthed and died. It is where the altar bench invited me to talk to God.

In the youth meeting I shared candidly about the mistakes I made and urged them to avoid such errors in judgment but instead to trust the Word of God, not people, or even my own emotions. With my young son sitting near me,

I confessed and cried and begged them to find out what God says and not what people say, not even preachers, but to cherish Proverbs 3:5-6, the verses I forgot in my youth. As I looked across the audience, I saw young people crying. They were struggling too.

The youth pastor and his wife, James and Vera Snow, took me under their wings. They helped me with babysitting and let me hang out at their house. James even taught me to make flavorful beef stew. He became my Dad of sorts during a time when I had no one else. He wasn't a preacher, just a good kind man.

Former co-worker Donnie Kuhn invited me to attend a New Year's Eve party with him. Donnie and I enjoyed several lunch dates in subsequent weeks. During one of those lunch dates, Donnie seemed preoccupied. He didn't order and seemed sad or anxious. Looking across the table with trembling lips, he said, "I don't want to go to hell."

After I finished work for the day, we went together to the McLoud Pentecostal Holiness Church where the most recent pastor waited. Donnie ran to the altar and wept. He cried aloud for forgiveness for everyone he ever hurt as well as for himself. Later, he said he had a vision while at the altar, a vision of an open book. He knew his name was in it.

We were both baptized, me for the second time in a real baptistry where there were no snakes.

Donnie and I talked about marriage, but I was not ready. After a sequence of breakups and reconciliations and my fear of making another commitment and failing again, Donnie gave up. After James Snow said I should marry Donnie, I called him and agreed to marry him. He made the official engagement during a beautiful romantic dinner. Even then, I felt unsure: unsure of what love really was and what commitment meant from both parties.

Donnie grew up in western Oklahoma where he worked the farm fields. His family moved to Del City when his Dad fought lung cancer. His roots loosened, but mine remained deeply intact in McLoud. I refused to move to Del City where he lived at the time, so he agreed to live in my town, McLoud.

We set the date for when we accumulated leave from Tinker Air Force Base. Donnie and I married October 10, 1974 in McLoud. The pastor believed individual circumstances allowed for the two of us to start again. So I did. I started over.

Shortly after Donnie and I married, he threw the checkbook down on the kitchen table and told me it was mine.

"Whatever we put in, use it to pay bills or spend for our family, but, you must tithe first." It was the first time I had my name on a checking account and the first time since I was in high school I had been allowed to tithe.

My high school business class lessons came in handy as I balanced the checkbook and made every dime count. At first, it was not difficult because both of us worked. He had savings removed to a separate account before the rest was placed in the checking account. I prayed every week on how to get through the unfamiliar financial territory of checks and balances.

The spring after Donnie and I married in October, a family member notified me that my ex-husband had been diagnosed with brain cancer. The prognosis did not look good because the tumor had been growing for approximately nine years. The headaches made sense then: his forgetfulness, accumulated unpaid bills, and impotence. Like a complicated, disorganized puzzle, the pieces suddenly fell into place. In a chasm of sadness I had never experienced, I tortured myself for not knowing, not being patient, not understanding. I saw myself through a dark lens. I wept.

After his brain surgery, my ex-husband and I met together to forgive each other. Marriage should have opened a path for each of us to bring out the best in each other, but instead was blocked by selfishly meeting our own individual emotional and financial needs.

Shortly after his death, I was awakened by his voice calling my name. I saw him standing near the bedroom door, the same place where I would be transported in the Spirit ten years later. He smiled. I accepted his eternal forgiveness and blessing. Forgiveness of myself and others cracked the hardened layer on my heart and life began to sprout.

Being forgiven and forgiving does not guarantee there will be no grief for that which has been lost. I grieved for lost relationship with him, his family, and his children. I grieved for my family, my parents and siblings who had entered into new lives where I no longer had place.

Self-doubt and unrealistic expectations of Donnie kept my heart at arms length. He did not sense a need to assure me of his love with the three little ones I craved to hear, I love you. I did not know what defined human love, how to receive it or how to give what did not truly exist in my own heart.

At one point, the emotional struggle in my soul caused me to think about taking my son and running away. I wanted out of life. I did not really know what I wanted, except I did not want to hurt any more. I did not want to fail any more. Like Dad, I wanted peace. I wanted to love and be loved, but I did not know what that looked like or felt like or how to reach inside myself and find it, because all the people I loved were like water in the desert that soaked away into dust. I understood love, like water, had to exist but it would take a lot of digging to find the source where it could be continually fed. Opening a clear, flowing channel of living water required blasting through years of accumulated emotional debris while trying to live with one foot on a strong pillar of faith and one foot on a constantly crumbling pillar of bad theology and human stubbornness. Mama and Dad must have been right. She told me often I was stubborn like my Dad. He said I was hard-headed like my mother. Surely, I inherited their natures which warred within me even with the new birth of spiritual awareness!

I took off work for the day. I washed dishes and asked God to help me get out of my short marriage. If God allowed me to get enough money, I promised to take my son to Africa and become a missionary, always the ultimate career, going far away to do something good for someone who would appreciate it. The answer was not what I expected.

The Holy Spirit spoke to my spirit, "Can you love someone in Africa who is going to kill your son?"

"Of course," I told the inner voice. "They would not know what they were doing.

"If you cannot love someone who is willing to share life with you and your son, how can you love someone who is a stranger?"

In my immature unawareness of the meaning of love, I cried to God, "I know you love Donnie, Lord, but I can't love him the way You love him. But, I will allow you to love him through me."

When Donnie arrived home that evening, my pre-planned verbal attack was ready. But, as I walked from the kitchen to greet him at the door, the only words that came from my mouth were, "I love you."

It surprised us both.

From that day when I became frustrated with the relationship, I would pray and ask God to change Donnie. Without exception, the Holy Spirit would teach me how I could change myself.

"You are always on his side," I cried out to God. I think I felt him smile.

Our marriage survived because I submitted to instructions from that inner voice. God was no longer someone I tried to please, but a friend I knew I could trust to tell me the truth about myself, even when I did not want to hear it.

I resigned from Tinker Air Force Base with a promise to Donnie that if he let me quit, I would do anything, even scrub toilets with a toothbrush. While the ink dried on my resignation paperwork and I said my final farewells to coworkers, my brother George sent word that Dad died.

About two years earlier, I had visited my Dad during the Christmas season. Before I left his little rented mobile home, I sat down on his lap, hugged him and told him I loved him, the first time I had uttered those words to him since I was a child. He pushed me off his lap and did not return the phrase. Love, as I saw it then, was not about whether a person's actions deserve to be loved; only on one's willingness to give it away in perpetuity.

My siblings and I decided to bury Dad in McLoud Riverside Cemetery located near the Johnie Chambless farm where we had picked blackberries as children. The cemetery was overgrown. The hog wire fence was bent and rusted. Pieces of discarded fake flowers, glass jars and downed tree limbs scattered the seven acres of carved granite engraved with names and numbers identifying people whose bodies lay beneath the red clay soil. In November 1975, the cemetery appeared as if no one mowed it all summer.

George, Bruce, James, and Donnie cleaned the cemetery the three days prior to a graveside service for our Dad. That was about how long it took my pregnant sister to arrive from North Carolina where her husband was stationed in the military. Dad has two stones on his grave, one from the veterans indicating he was born in 1926 and one accurate stone indicating he was born in 1927. All untruths will ultimately be exposed. Dad lied about his age to get in the U.S. Marine Corps, but death stripped all fallacy away.

The next spring I stood at the entrance of the cemetery and decided I could either mow Dad's grave and keep it nice or try to work out something where everyone buried there could lie peacefully in a maintained honorarium. I decided to take on the big task. Donnie and I mowed that spring, which began our thirty-year commitment to caring for the grounds.

The February after Daddy died, my four-year-old son, Gary, came into the kitchen as I cooked.

"I want a baby brother or sister," he said.

Without considering my answer, I replied, "We will pray God will give us one like he gave us you."

"Let's pray right now," he said.

In the seconds I thought it through, I decided if I prayed with him and nothing happened, his faith might be hindered. After all, I trusted the doctors and bore scars to prove I had already lost one ovary and the other might be damaged. If I did not pray with him, he would know I did not have faith. He was four years old, too young to understand the surgeries and limitations of infertility. I could pray with him and he might forget about the prayer when he played with his toys again. I led him to his favorite coffee table where he did most of his art and put together his molded plastic towers. We knelt by the 1950s-model, blond-colored table left over from the old trailer we lived in, and prayed a simple prayer. He returned to playing, and I returned to preparing lunch. It was February.

In April, I felt very tired and sleepy. One day a friend came to check on me and asked if I was pregnant.

"No, I don't think so," I said, confident of a prognosis that I would never be able to have children.

Tiredness swaddled me. Finally, I drove to the Pottawatomie County Health Department for a free pregnancy test, just in case my friend was right. The nurse said I was pregnant. Unemotional at first, I absorbed the news. Remembering my gynecologists words that even if I became pregnant, I couldn't carry a baby to term, I made an appointment to go see him in two weeks.

On December 9, 1976, I delivered a son Gregory Don, an eight-pound, six-ounce baby boy after three hours of labor.

During the pregnancy, I attended a weekly quilting group at the church, the same group of ladies who quilted for missions when I was growing up. They were older now but still faithful to quilt for missions and fellowship with each other centered on a healthy lunch and a Bible lesson.

A female evangelist holding a series of revival meetings, visited the quilting group one week. We ate a big lunch, all sitting around the table as she talked about praying for what we needed. I stated I believed we should do as much as we could on the little things in life then ask God to help with what we could not handle. She pointed her bony finger at me, steeled her brown eyes into mine and said, "If you don't trust God for the little things, you will not trust him for the big things."

Her words took me aback. She was right: the little foxes spoil the vines. Every mountain is made up of grains of sand

and every plant grows from a small seed. Taking her correction to heart, I disciplined my prayer life to trust God for the small things, like grocery money, sore muscles, wise choices and the larger picture, like children to one barren.

As I prayed in the den one day while the children rested, I asked the Lord what He wanted me to do to earn money. I really wanted to be home with my boys, but financially, that would be difficult for our family. After I quit work, the road narrowed and the river of income became a trickle. I entertained the idea of going to college again. I saved the three-thousand dollars retirement when I resigned from Tinker for college, but the amount hardly handled the first year. I heard about a licensed practical nursing program at Gordon Cooper Technology Center in Shawnee. After calculating a budget, I concluded the money covered one year with costs of gasoline, books, and tuition, if accepted into the program. The Center accepted me, and I graduated at the top of my class, taking a day-shift position in the newborn nursery of a Shawnee hospital. It was my joy to assist with women giving birth, coaching them through their delivery process, and teaching them how to care for their babies at home.

Chapter 15
Brother John

"I am reminded of your sincere faith, which first lived in your grandmother Lois and in your mother Eunice and, I am persuaded, now lives in you also." II Timothy 1:5 NIV

"I love you," he said.

My mind went into a tailspin. My stomach lurched.

This is not possible, I thought as I walked away more calmly than my insides felt. *My God, how did he misunderstand my church attendance as personal affection?*

While the pastor never offered inappropriate attention, his words reverberated in my ears. Now, the second Sunday in a little church, and already a stranger told me he loved me. I could not comprehend the meaning of his words. Not one pastor ever told me that either he or God loved me personally. God loved good church people, but me?

Reason set in.

After all, I thought, *he said it in front of God and everybody, right there in the church lobby. Maybe he meant it innocently. Maybe.*

I turned and noticed he told everyone he loved them as they passed by to shake his outstretched hand.

What was love? I needed to answer this question in my mind.

Love was mercurial.

Love was sometimes suspended when behavior did not match the ideals of the one expressing love.

Love was guarded in a heart so deeply, I concluded no one could express it correctly.

Love was an evolution from introduction to like to care to affirmed sincerity, which it may not withstand.

"Love" could mean anything from sexual love to enjoying a raisin oatmeal cookie with a warm cup of tea, to regarding exercise as a daily stimulant, or even being addicted to the feeling of carefreeness.

I did not say "I love you" often. My parents rarely used those triune words together to each other or to us. My grandparents did not say them to me because it was understood by their unconditional acceptance. I used those words with Dad when he was drunk, to make him comply, not because he was acting lovingly. So, what motivated an acquaintance to use that three-syllable selection of the English language? I chewed on it all week. Searching my memory bank for any innuendoes, I found nothing but kindness from Pastor John who reflected human value wrapped in common faith.

I decided to be bold and say it back to him, just to convince myself I could say "I love you" to a man who was not my husband or father or grandfather in a non-intrusive, asexual way. I craved the freedom to tell someone I loved them without it being taken as a license to mistreat me or as a sexual overture. I knew the power of love but had not experienced the freedom of expressing it without being misunderstood. By Sunday, all the fear was crammed into a cartridge just below the breastbone. As people eased out of the church, I waited my turn. My heart raced. I wasn't sure I could do it. Easing my sons ahead of me, I reached for the pastor's big carpenter-like hand, looking into his smiling face and eyes that valued me as a dad would his daughter, and waited. He said, "I love you, Sis."

"I love you, too," like a trigger my voice exploded, echoing off the concrete block walls of the little building. I said it. I crossed the line. I was now free to say, "I love you," in a platonic relationship. Wisdom tempered it in time, but the cat was out of the bag, the bird out of the cage, and agape set free.

My path to the little Assembly of God Church was a winding one.

"Get me out of here before I die!" I cried out to God after a very discouraging Sunday night service in the McLoud Pentecostal Holiness Church. I was hungry for more of God, but the church of my childhood served up condemnation like Sunday pot roast. I could no longer bear the burden of measuring up.

A small Assembly of God Church south of McLoud closed shortly after I graduated high school, but I heard it re-opened. So, one Sunday night I left the boys home with Donnie and visited. About five people were in the congregation; the pastor and his wife made seven. Brother John, as the pastor introduced himself, was a large-framed, balding man with a kind, toothy smile. His wife, Wanda, played piano. Her raven black hair and bright blue eyes, contrasted nicely with her beautiful creamy complexion. She was quick to welcome everyone. I found the music nice and the sermon interesting.

Later the following week as I watered plants, I noticed two women walking. One woman saw me and waved. I waved back. As I continued my yard work, the ladies made the corner and walked into the driveway. It was Wanda and a friend. I found her willingness to open the windows of community and invite individuals in refreshing. Because of her visit, I took my family to the Assembly of God Church the following Sunday and never returned to the Pentecostal Holiness Church.

Shortly after we began attending the church, Brother John Cuzick taught a lesson on the four Greek words for love in the New Testament. I made notes in my red Bible. *Eros*, is the sexual attraction expressed within a spousal relationship. *Storge'* is family love. *Phile'* is a brotherly and sisterly relationship. And *agape'* is to give extreme value, as God values people unconditionally.

Like the sun, love has impacted all humanity throughout eons. Love knows only the limits placed by the recipient, for the Creator (from which love originates) is undiluted by time or space in pure agape'. Yet the English language made no distinction between types of love, and I unsuccessfully tried to form lumps of similar but dissected clays into one incomprehensible group.

Brother John was a disciplinarian pastor. His kindness provided the necessary ointment to the Brillo pad message of prescribed living he preached. Every Sunday I left church feeling like I needed to change my attitude about relationships, and lifestyle choices. Every preconceived idea on godly living had to be reconsidered in light of God's Word. As Paul the Apostle wrote, I needed my mind renewed, so I could see clearly the love of God and His love for humanity.

Discipleship, I decided, was much like scraping layers of barnacles from the hidden underbelly of a ship. Only God's Word cuts through experience-hardened selfishness to expose basic human nature so it can be cleansed. Only then can the Master Artist of humanity begin to reveal His purpose with each stroke of His divine masterpiece on the born-again human heart. It took years and hard work to change old thought processes, but it must be done. Because God loved me, I wanted to please Him. Because I wanted to please Him, I needed to know how to do it. Like a newly-married bride learning to join her life with her husband, I was ready to learn day by day how to walk in unity with the One to whom I surrendered my spirit. When I became frustrated and discouraged, the voice would comfort me.

In this season, life revolved around me and Jesus, but Brother John broadened my vision. John Cuzick joined the

McLoud City Council. He assisted with the Cub Scout program and pinned Gary for his progress in Scouting. He hugged our sons weekly and baptized Gary after he made a personal commitment to Christ.

One Sunday after church service Pastor John handed me a book, *Mission of Mercy,* the story of Mark and Hulda Buntain, missionaries to India. The Buntains took children off the streets of Calcutta, fed them, educated them, and trained them for jobs and service. Their faith and hard work resulted in giving life to thousands of unwanted children. Through their diligence to serve, they constructed a hospital where children were treated, then later trained in the medical profession. There had been other influential books in my earlier journey, those by WWII survivor Corrie Ten Boom, and David Wilkerson, and a book entitled *God's Smuggler* by John and Elizabeth Sherrill. *God's Smuggler* chronicled the events of Brother Andrew who smuggled bibles into the Soviet Union.

I found a card at the end of *Mission of Mercy* where a person could commit to sponsoring a child for twenty dollars a month at the Buntain's organization. Remembering the commitment made by the ladies who quilted to support missions, I also made the commitment to sponsor a child.

Living agape' was budding. The organization assigned a girl to us. Shortly after we sponsored her, I received a note from Mission of Mercy saying she left the school for unexplained reasons, so they assigned me a young boy named Elvis Wynters. My family sponsored Elvis until he graduated. Through those years, I continued locally to teach Sunday school, lead singing, or anything else I could put my hands and heart to doing for the people, doing it because I learned love is an active word.

John's sermons helped me realize that my past could not cloud a renewed mind. I must win a war day by day against condemnation. Like dental plaque, past failures and false beliefs about who God is and what is required to know Him needed to be continually chipped away before a healthy spiritual relationship could grow. John's teaching of God's Word with no additives and seasoned with agape' love allowed me to understand the reality of inner freedom and spiritual responsibility.

Brother John taught his congregation to pray. He didn't hold a seminar because his life was a training program. He arrived before church to pray. Having the gift of speaking in tongues, he prayed in his spiritual language and with his understanding. He walked and prayed. He knelt and prayed.

He exhorted each person in his congregation to pray. But, he allowed each member of the church to develop their own communication frequency as each individual adapted a path to follow Jesus' instructions on prayer.

Under his leadership, I changed, growing in faith, studying the Word, throwing off the weights that bound me. The voice returned. Instead of speaking occasionally, I heard it in my dreams and daily life, encouraging me, correcting me, teaching me, leading me. In prayer once again I saw faces of people for whom I could pray. When I went to the mall shopping, I found myself praying for strangers I passed. I also prayed for those from my past, and for my assigned patients at the hospital where I worked.

My nursing career had broadened. I worked evenings and tried to go to classes in preparation for my Registered Nursing degree. But, mother-hood, college, and a demanding profession began to take its toll on me physically. I had a second ovary removed. It also had become cystic. I was anemic again. Knowing I could return to nursing after finishing my degree, I took a much needed break to heal. I planned to return to school in two years. As I left the hospital the last day, I saw a sign announcing a woman evangelist was holding a revival. It was the same lady evangelist who had stuck her finger in my face and told me I should trust God in the little things, a reminder I needed to place my trust in His divine plan for me. God's timing amazed me.

Brother John and Wanda later moved from McLoud with instructions for me to keep teaching the Word of God to people in the church.

"I am leaving them in your care," he said.

The Cuzick's leaving McLoud created a hole in our church and our family. They unloaded most of their personal belongings to go to a small town in southwest Oklahoma before making the giant leap to Jamaica, where they served for several years. John and Wanda settled in the Washington D.C. area, assisting with an International congregation. From time to time John sent me a book he thought I would like. I wrote a letter on occasion. In the years since, I have never had a pastor who taught me so much in a short time, not just with his words, but by living and loving people.

As my family changed because of the dedication of this pastor and the incidental gift of a book, India would be changed by the little boy we sponsored with twenty dollars a month until he graduated. The Lord allowed us to meet

Elvis so I could hear the rest of his story and so I should share how reaching out to him taught me the unlimited agape' love of God.

As I noted previously, forty is the biblical number representing testing. As I neared my fortieth birthday, I sensed I had emerged. There was a trickle of life flowing from my inner being. Expectation was rising. But, there was more to come, more than I could have ever imagined.

Chapter 16
Tasting the Visions

"But in your hearts revere Christ as Lord. Always be prepared to give an answer to everyone who asks you to give the reason for the hope that you have. But do this with gentleness and respect." I Peter 3: 15 NIV

After the Cuzick's left the McLoud church, I was trying to teach the adult Sunday school class. Realizing I did not know as much as I should, I enrolled in a six-trimester satellite Bible training program at a church in Shawnee. While the boys were in school, I was able to attend classes. Teaching became easy then, because all I had to do was share what I was learning from some of the best acclaimed Bible teachers of the time. The Word amazed me. Truths I was learning were establishing my faith and maximizing my devotion to God's plan for mankind. Understanding formed from the biblical narratives.

In my Bible study time, I had begun writing the inspirations I gained. I entitled my devotionals, A Personal Touch.

I stopped in at *The McLoud News* to ask if they would like to publish some of my articles. The owners added A Personal Touch to their weekly setup. In 1986 after completing Bible and Leadership training, the owners asked if I would like to cover local meetings. I was hired to also help with typing, layout and design of the weekly newspaper for a minimal salary. On Tuesday evenings, I assisted with layout on stand-up boards, just like those I had seen when visiting an area newspaper in the fourth grade. At some point I I began to realize the vision of every door in McLoud opening up to me as I embedded myself more and more into the life and lives of the community.

Since it was only part-time work, I devoted myself to prayer at home and to study to teach Sunday school classes.

It was during this time, I had a the three-day spiritual journey.

By the time the newspaper owner's wife died of lung cancer, I had accepted most of the weekly process of producing the newspaper.

Before new growth can sprout, unproductive branches must be removed. Radical pruning began. Turning loose is painful. Being cut loose is traumatic.

A newly appointed pastor at McLoud First Assembly of God misunderstood my passion for teaching the Bible. I was approached by a member of the Board of the Church and told I should step down from all service in the church. A reference made about my emotional instability reminded me of Mama's threats to put me in a mental institution. It was a quick unexpected action with which I was cut away from my spiritual support.

My family began to attend a non-denominational congregation at Life Christian Center. Dwight Burchett was the pastor.

The newspaper owner remarried and sold to new owners. I stayed in the McLoud office where I continued to put out the weekly publication with much help from a great team. Ricky Sanders reported and photographed sports, Mary took care of accounting, and Glenda S. became a productive advertising representative. I became involved in all aspects of the community and the process of putting out the weekly news. Reporting local news was more than a business for me. It was a spiritual calling.

One day my friend and prayer partner, Nelly Burris invited me to accompany her to Lugano, Switzerland. It was

1989 when I requested leave for ten days to accompany my friend to her home town.

Nelly and I met at an outdoor evangelism crusade in McLoud when her youngest of six children was just a baby and my youngest was about eight-years-old. She and her husband David and their family became close friends. Nelly had two sisters and a brother in Switzerland, along with nieces and nephews. She tried to make a trip to see family there about every two years.

After talking with Donnie about going away for a couple of weeks, he agreed I should go. My passport arrived just in time. Nelly made all the travel arrangements because I had never traveled outside the U.S., except a short trip to Mexico.

From the hub in Atlanta, the plane carried us up the Eastern Seaboard. From my window seat, I could look down on the continent's east side where the earth met water. I watched the lights of Nova Scotia twinkle hello as the plane carried us over the edge of Canada. Nelly said I should sleep, but I could not. I was living the first act of the three-day vision near the door of my bedroom. While some passengers pulled on night blinders, cuddling beneath thin airline blankets, I stood near the bulkhead where I looked out of the porthole-sized window frame and saw the lights of Iceland, Ireland and later Britain before landing in Frankfurt, Germany. My sense was that I had landed on another planet. I did not understand anything anyone said, except Nelly. After a layover, we boarded the last leg of the flight, but not the end of the journey.

From Zurich, we stepped onto a train for Lugano, Switzerland. My brain cried for sleep. My body ached from tiredness, but I could not close my eyes. I wanted to see everything, the little garden spots along the train tracks, the geraniums floating from window boxes perched on the rail of verandas beneath peaked dark, brown-sided roofs. Cows scattered in the meadows, chewing the cud, relaxed, their bodies creating milk for thirsty children. Small villages dotted the travel route in front of the constant backdrop of snow-packed mountain peaks. The train finally eased to a gentle stop in Lugano where Nelly's sister, Lilly, awaited our arrival. She wore a light blue dress and sandals. Her blond hair coordinated perfectly with her peach complexion. I relaxed. This was not a vision. This was really happening.

Nelly and Lilly were so excited to see each other. They chattered quickly in Swiss-Italian. My brain and body were numb. When we arrived at Lilly's apartment, I slept immediately and deeply.

For the remainder of the trip, I easily prayed from my heart as I entered the life where my friend grew up. One day, during our stay in Switzerland, we took a day to travel by bus to Venice by way of Milan. Venice was crowded with people walking the boardwalk area. I strolled leisurely. Nelly reminded me to move faster or the crowd would worm its way between us and I could get lost. But, I wanted to drink in the atmosphere of the real city, the one I peeked into between the buildings that egressed from the boardwalk.

I wanted to consume into my memory the beautiful ceramics and glassware displayed in storefronts through which generations had dreamed, as if I was one of the people who lived in and loved this city. I wanted to meet the people of Venice, not its visitors. Gondoliers pushed small boats carrying tourists along canals of unknown depth. A tour guide was overheard telling his passengers the city of Venice was sinking, being dragged by currents and gravity to its reclamation by the ocean from which it came. Standing there eavesdropping on his explanation to tourists, I began to consider life based on the beautiful city of Venice fading away at some future date. Remembering the crow of my childhood, I understood that all living things, seek to return to their original state. A wild creature will crave its freedom; a dammed stream will seek its flow; the sea will pull at the claimed piers sucking them back into its bosom.

During our stay in Switzerland, we visited many ancient churches in large cities and small villages. Some no longer held Christian services but were monuments to past spiritual experiences. Most were Catholic churches complete with pews, kneeling boards, and a large crucifix of the dying Christ. Some had stained glass windows depicting biblical stories and icons of heroes of the Christian faith dotting the windowsills. A few had ornately painted ceilings faded by age and the light of many candles. On a day trip to Northern Italy for shopping, I noticed a tiny church tucked into a small opening from the main market pathway. A priest at the door welcomed guests. I pointed out the church to Nelly, who asked if I wanted to go see it, which I did.

As we approached the open church door, the young priest stood to the side and welcomed us into the sanctuary with a broad smile and a sweep of his hand. Something felt unusual about the small church. People smiled at each other as they made their way to light candles or kneel before the altar area. Nelly and I enjoyed the old stained glass depictions as we made our way to the altar. Instead of a crucifix of Jesus Christ dying on the cross, the altar held a bright golden cast of a risen Jesus Christ, astride a horse, holding a standard of victory. It sent the message that Jesus Christ was no longer on the cross, but had risen from the dead and would return victorious over all the enemies of God. The priest was filled with vitality, his kind greetings expressed through his radiant eyes and hearty hand-shakes. This momentary visit to this small church continues to remind me to continually consider whether Christ is dying or living in my heart.

Nelly escorted me to the mountain village where she attended school and church during her early childhood. Lilly was with us. We spent the night in an ancient home nestled there in the Alps.

Nelly's nephew took us to eat the last evening of our stay at a nice little restaurant in Lugano. After the meal, he toasted his Aunt Nelly and I with a clear liquid in a small jigger. Giovanni insisted I toast and sip. Not wanting to offend, I took one sip, enough to set my throat into a violent cough. I smelled enough of Dad's alcohol to know I wouldn't like the taste, and I didn't. Giovanni and his friends laughed gleefully. My welcome to the Swiss family was sealed with a sip.

Mostly I sipped cappuccino, but little to no water or juice. The Chernobyl nuclear accident occurred a few months before our trip to Nelly's home country, and National Media was warning everyone not to drink the water because winds carried the nuclear fallout throughout Europe. Because juice was so expensive, I was reluctant to drink it when offered. I did drink my cappuccino, which tasted like strong coffee clouded with sweet cream. Small wonder they served it in such small amounts. Cappuccino did little to satisfy my thirst but much to boost my energy level.

Unlike the humidity of Oklahoma, summer air in Switzerland and Italy dehydrated me. Due to my reluctance to drink juice and water by the time we flew back to the United States, I was severely dehydrated. When the stewardess asked if I wanted something to drink, I asked for water, lots of it. At one point, I asked her if she could leave the pitcher. She did not but hovered over me with water for the remainder of the trip. As a seasoned traveler, she obviously recognized my craving for water.

With my first step in Europe, I crossed a border that kept me confined to the Western Hemisphere. My friend Nelly held my hand for the first leap across the ocean in neutral surroundings. Not knowing whether I would cross the ocean again, I prayed for the countries I visited to be blessed with wise leadership and kind people. Though I knew little about the effects of radiation on the environment, I prayed for the people of Chernobyl, Ukraine, who were cast quickly into an ocean of foul air; their families and nearby countries receiving the caustic fall-out. I prayed for the land to heal and bring forth crops again. And I prayed for those who remained shuttered behind the iron fist of communism.

Many before me prayed for these things. I simply joined my small voice in the cantata of prayer made up of millions.

Transversing the Atlantic was not the beginning of my life in the earth, but it seemed like a new beginning of sorts. I was forty-one when I traveled to Switzerland with my friend. It seemed the vision had prepared me to look back to what I had learned the first forty years of my life in the earth and forward to my destiny.

God's grace had prepared me and brought me to this place at His designated time.

I returned to newspaper work with an expanded world view. Then, suddenly, without warning, that branch too was pruned.

Chapter 17
To Russia With Love

"See, I will bring them from the land of the north and gather them from the ends of the earth."
Jeremiah 31:8, NIV

In November 1989, a few months after Nelly and I traveled to Switzerland, the Berlin Wall came tumbling down. What lay behind the wall astonished the world and opened a fifty-year cultural time capsule.

As the de facto capital city of the German Democratic Republic, East Berlin was formally the Soviet sector as established in 1945. Residents of East Berlin lived separated from their West Berlin community by what became known as the iron curtain, I had learned about in junior high school. No one could predict how long the passage between east and west would remain open. The immediate effect was that of a tidal wave of new products and services sweeping into the gaping market and social hole where dry bones of economically and socially confined humanity had been trapped in a silent desert.

Evangelists from every Christian denomination poured into East Germany. News organizations set up stations to alert the world. Churches prepared to plant their theology. After decades of sneaking Bibles to the underground church, enduring limbs cut off during interrogations, living in cramped inhumane prisons for their faith, Christian believers were once again free to openly share their faith. Like spring iris bulbs, Christians driven into the darkness to protect their faith emerged stronger than those who lived in freedom.

A break in the wall meant an open door for commerce. People living within its iron grip found themselves plunged into a brisk freshwater cistern filled with wonderful commodities shared by sharks on feeding frenzies. An array of fast food companies quickly made plans to establish new enterprises offering flavors to tantalize the appetites of a new generation. Shipping containers filled with treasures from around the world came to ports ready for distribution to the vast new northern Russian market. Industrialists poured into the country hoping to reopen closed factories or build new ones. In the chaos of economic emergence, vice sneaked behind the curtain too, luring the young and innocent with sickeningly seductive not yet illegal drugs.

The spring of 1991, co-owners of *The McLoud News* cut out my one-third partnership. The move came unexpectedly without warning.

In October 1991, I was invited to become an administrative assistant to Pastor Dwight Burchett of Life Christian Center. It was part time, but it helped me earn tuition for our youngest son who needed to leave McLoud schools.

In the Fall of 1993, a co-worker at the church stepped up to my desk, peered over my computer and casually asked, "Would you like to go to Russia with me?"

"Sure," I said it without hesitation. After discussing it with Donnie, we finalized our plans. Dot Eden and I boarded a plane in Oklahoma City. It was April 1994.

There I was on a dirty Russian train going somewhere into the darkness. Dot and I were specks in a dust storm formed by thousands from around the world wanting to leverage a break in the Berlin Wall to the land of Khrushchev and Lenin.

I lay wide awake on a filthy, dark Russian train. My traveling companion, Dot, and I stayed in the same berth with two men from our missions team: Alex from Canada seemed to be the leader of our four-member team and a Gomer Pyle lookalike, whose name I do not remember, from Tennessee. I watched the splotchy, blackened snow through the small, smudged train window and wondered what I was doing in Russia, away from my family, in this train traveling out of Moscow to who knows where. With orders not to leave the berth without contacting our translator, I wanted more than anything to be back in Oklahoma.

In the darkness, I rehearsed the journey thus far.

It had been a harrowing forty-eight hours. Our plane took off from Oklahoma City and we met up with a group in Chicago. The second plane to Amsterdam was delayed due to mechanical problems. I thanked God that the mechanics found the problem before we streamed over the North Atlantic. After about five hours at the gate, I felt frantic we would miss subsequent connections. Part of me teased a hope the plane would not fly at all so I could go back home. A small group of team members went into a deserted area of the O'Hare International Airport, joined hands, and prayed. Shortly thereafter, the announcement over the intercom said we were ready to leave.

We arrived in Moscow late in the night in a small, dented, and aged Russian tin-can of a plane. It was the end of the flight, but our journey was just beginning. The next eight-hour leg by train took us away from Moscow to a large military city, Orel. Gathering our luggage, Dot and I set out by van with four strangers: Alex, "Gomer", translator Dema, and a burly driver.

Dot's luggage was not among the suitcases loaded in the van because it was inadvertently delivered to another team. I am sure Dot and I would have rolled our eyes if we could have seen each other in the old van traveling through pot-holed, garbage-strewn dark streets toward the train station. Instead, we held armrests as the van maneuvered past closed storefronts. Occasional dim yellow street lights added an eerie feel to the city. Small lumps of dirty snow lay along the curbside. Glimpses of men lying in the entrances of apartment buildings hinted the van may have entered a meandering homeless camp. We did not know then another more venomous gauntlet awaited, more than yellow lights and sleeping drunks.

We needed sleep, but there would not be any for a while.

When the driver stopped near what appeared to be a speaker from an old drive-in theater, we pulled our luggage out, except Dot's.

A translator, two male team members, two strangers dressed in grubby coats, and our driver assisted with luggage, as we moved slowly over the dark terraced ground where splotches of snow refused to melt. Together the group stumbled and collided with suitcases toward a dimly lit, glass-enclosed area, apparently the train station.

As we approached the glass doors, five men wearing camouflage carrying assault rifles over their shoulders and belts of ammo around their waists confronted our translator. Dema talked to them for a while before telling us in English, the men demanded a bribe to enter the train station. Each man in our small group pulled out Russian rubles. Dot and I had not exchanged money. As the five men counted the paper money, we rushed past them through the doors to buy tickets. Speeding toward the train platform, everyone but Dot pulling too-heavy, too-full luggage toward the elevated platform, we glimpsed our assigned smudge-covered massive iron train. Doors slid open. We boarded, men first so they could pull up luggage. Dema urged us to hurry. As I looked back toward the station, I saw the men in camouflage, pushing through the second set of glass doors between the ticket space and the train. They ran toward us. Before my head could fully return to the open train door, the two men from our group grasped my hands and pulled me onto the train. The doors shut just as a camouflage-clad man reached the entry.

We rushed to our four-bed berth where we all collapsed from relief and exhaustion with gratefulness the gauntlet had been scaled.

I slept soundly for a while on the jostling train. I did not open the door. Dema told us not to open it for any reason. If we needed a bathroom break, we should bang on the wall behind the top bunk where Alex slept. The toilet was actually a hole in the train floor, so I had no desire to go there. Our translator occupied the next berth and would come for us.

When the train arrived in Orel, sunshine greeted us along with another young man who Dema introduced as Andrew. He acknowledged us with a slight nod but said nothing. We carried luggage, too much luggage, to a waiting van. Dema told Dot her luggage would be brought the next day. From where he did not say. Actually, I didn't even know where Orel was in relation to Moscow. The black and white movie set I sensed I had entered kept me watching for a yellow-brick road to show me the way out or an Oz to approach for help. In the drabness of late April in Russia, yellow would have been a welcome contrast.

The van rolled up to an out-of-the-way cottage which appeared more like a sprawling one-story attachment of progressive structures. When we arrived in Moscow, Alex told us to keep our passports on us at all times, so I was confused when Dema told me that the owner of the Russian bed and breakfast would take necessary documents overnight for security purposes. Reluctantly, I handed mine over with everyone else, with Dema's assurance it was required and would be safe. As we passed through one section of the house into the living room, a group of elderly men and women sat around what appeared to be a 1950s-model black and white television set watching Nikita Khrushchev give a speech. I recognized the file footage from my junior high school years in McLoud, during the Cold War. I sensed I walked deeper into a fifty-year time capsule and prayed I would return from its iron bowels.

Two twin beds in the small room Dot and I shared appeared clean. Dema suggested we freshen up before dinner in the dining room. Wary eyes again followed our walk through the television room and into an adjacent smaller dining room with the 1950s-curtained windows where waiters served us mashed potatoes, cabbage, and bread. This was the first meal of many with those three ingredients.

After cold showers, because warm water was only available during specific hours, Dot and I collapsed on the thin mattresses and embraced the first sound sleep since leaving Oklahoma.

After a quick breakfast of tea and bread the next morning, we went to a school for the blind. Our passports were not ready to be returned, but Dema assured us we would be fine. "Fine" to me meant possessing my passport again, but I was at the mercy of strangers in a foreign country of people who spoke a different language. On the way to the school for the blind, the van driver stopped beside a stop sign and opened the door. Andrew hopped on, spoke to Dema, and hopped off at the next stop. Andrew followed this pattern throughout our time in Orel. Dema then gave instructions to the driver and the van pulled into the light, slow traffic.

We traveled to the school for the blind, gave out some gifts and Dema translated short speeches of greetings. When we returned to the bus, Dema announced we could not stay in the same cottage where our passports were held. We would return to get our luggage and passports and he would find another place for the five of us to stay.

We retrieved our luggage but not our passports. Dema said Andrew would take care of it. Meanwhile, we went to the next meeting, an orphanage.

Conditions in the orphanage were deplorable. Children sat or lay on bare metal-fenced mattresses, some urine-soaked. Big pleading, hollow eyes followed us as we made our way through small rooms housing about six children each. Some children were naked, even older challenged children wore only a cloth diaper. None smiled. Some reached out to us, but Dema told us not to touch them. Photography was not allowed. We brought gifts for those who could color or paint, which appeared to me to be none. The sponsoring organization sent funds through Dema to buy food, diapers, and soap for the orphanage. He and Alex brought those items to the administrator, who in turn handed them a list of things she wanted on the next trip to Orel. We left all the donations in the administrator's office who distributed them to those who could use them, or to their own children, or to sell them through the black market. We had no way of knowing for sure.

The bus driver seemed lost as he slowly drove around Orel. At a traffic light, the bus door opened and Andrew jumped on. He handed us our passports. I hugged it to my chest. I could breathe again.

The driver meandered the streets turning slowly into residential tunnels between high-rise apartment buildings reaching to touch clouds. He then pulled into the short half-moon drive of a high-rise apartment building. Young children sat on the cracked curb hitting sticks on the drive. Dot and I disembarked and gave the children Russian language gospel tracts. As the bus pulled away, we saw them reading the tracts. I entertained the idea I traveled to Russia for a reason. But the bus stopped suddenly on the other end of the half-moon drive. Dema announced we would stay in this "hotel" for the remainder of our trip.

As we entered the lobby, we presented our passports but no one required us to leave them. Dema escorted Dot and me to a small room with two twin beds and only a narrow aisle between, enough room for our legs and feet if we sat at opposite ends. The floors were stained. The beds were covered in clean, but old linens. The odor was not bad, just stale.

After depositing my luggage, Dot and I joined Alex in the hallway, hoping he could direct us to a restaurant or a vending machine. While foraging for food, Alex said Russia didn't have vending machines and our hotel was a brothel. The hotel did not sell food, so we ate what we brought with us. Only tea could be purchased at the hotel. We heated water for tea to a boil in a small pot I brought with me. We were not to drink anything else. Bottled water would be distributed later. Trail mix and nutrition bars never tasted so good.

Dot and I ran into Alex in the hallway again the next morning. He stayed up most of the night talking with two hostesses at the brothel, telling them about Jesus Christ. Each acknowledged Jesus as their Savior. I hoped to see them again to meet them and welcome them into the family of God. We did not see them a second time.

While on the way to our next venue, during a quick traffic light stop, Andrew stepped inside and dropped Dot's luggage on the bus. Doors closed and he disappeared again.

On our third day, we went to what appeared to be an old theater with a stage in front. I wondered why small children were not in school, but I was happy they came. We gave testimonies of our relationship with Christ, sang songs with motions, and passed out a few gifts. The children wanted photographs with everyone, so we took as many as we could take before it was time to leave with promises of a return from Alex. I brought a Polaroid camera and a slew of film, so a photograph became a popular gift to leave with families.

Back on the bus, Alex explained that Orel is known as both a prison and military city. Our team would visit three prisons: one for youthful male offenders, one for men, and one for women. We visited the prison for youthful offenders first.

When the bus stopped, Alex and Dema led us into a small auditorium. Skinny young men with shaven heads came into the room, a living reminder of photos I had seen of Holocaust victims during World War II. I found it impossible to stop making the comparison of what I saw in front of me and the images of Jews in concentration camps. My heart ached at the sight of these young men and boys dressed in baggy black-and-white striped clothes, many arrested for stealing food, we were told. They diverted their eyes from us. Somehow I expected one to look up at me and cry, "Mama." Some of the youngest "offenders" in my estimation appeared to be about eight while others looked as old as eighteen. I could not accurately guess ages because of the obvious malnutrition. Some of the older prisoners put their arms around younger prisoners and whispered to them, patting them lovingly. The youngest prisoners appeared sad, maybe a bit frightened. Most kept their heads bowed as a guard led them to seats on bare-wood benches.

Andrew brought cases of Bibles on one of his unexpected appearances while the bus sat at a traffic stop. The man from Tennessee gave his testimony first with Dema translating. Then Dot and I greeted the young men. Alex gave a short teaching on Jesus Christ, His life, and resurrection. We laid Bibles on a table in front of the stage and invited the prisoners to take one.

We prayed and returned to the bus for the next venue. As we moved through Orel, my mind ventured to what I could do to help these prisoners know the Lord. Scriptures reminding all believers that faith without works is dead, revolved in my brain. "What can I do for them, Lord?" I prayed.

In a jolting afternoon journey through terraced pastureland, the team and translator rumbled toward the women's prison. Alex announced I would share the message. Yikes! I had nothing prepared. Noisy groans from my stomach reminded me of the change of my diet: potatoes, cabbage, horse meat, and some beets plus the stress of speaking to an audience. So, I prayed for wisdom to know what the ladies needed to hear and for my stomach to be quiet.

We went to a large common room with a small platform in front. I could not believe I was to speak. What could a girl from Oklahoma tell women destined to spend the rest of their lives incarcerated in a cold Russian prison?

Women prisoners slowly came into the room. Most tucked their heads down on their chest raising only their eyes as they made their way to a seat. A few raised their chins to the rafters in firm defiance, lowering their eyes to watch where they were going. The chin seemed to define the attitude among them.

Once they were seated, the warden introduced us. Each team member greeted the crowd. Then I went to the microphone. I did what the apostles did in the book of Acts: shared with them what Jesus had done for me. A ten-minute talk became twenty with translation. I shared that I was the daughter of a Christian mother and a loving Dad who began drinking when I was about ten years old. They understood my mother's struggle as they heard how she worked hard to raise us with very little money. The conclusion included emphasizing how faith in Jesus Christ and His resurrection brought us through those difficult years. I told them my Dad also submitted his spirit to Christ before his early death. I tried to look every person in the eye as I explained God loved each person so much He gave His Son so those who believed could have a relationship with a Heavenly Father, a Father who would never abandon them. It was a short and simple message.

As I shared my story and concluded with an invitation to accept Jesus Christ as Savior, I noticed chins either raising and lowering, depending on the attitude. Tears appeared in the eyes of some listeners. One woman stood and slowly came forward. Other women walked toward me. Some simply requested prayer, so we prayed with them. Some only wanted a Bible while others wanted to commit their lives to Jesus Christ. The warden and a helper assisted with passing out Bibles loaded by Andrew at an intersection. Some prisoners related their own stories in Russian. Dema tried to translate for selected ones, so I could only smile and weep, and hug and promise to pray signing by folding my hands.

When the head warden instructed the women to return to the prison area, one prisoner refused to leave us. She appeared to be in her early forties with bright black hair pulled into a bun at the base of her neck. She wore pants with legs that snuggled her calves, a heavy black and white coat, and blue shoes.

Gypsy? Maybe, I thought. *Did Gypsies live in Russia?* I would need to look that up. The warden could not deter her. She followed us to the gate in the fence near the bus. As Dema followed us to the bus, he could finally translate what she was trying to make me understand.

She made one request: "Please do not forget me!"

"I won't."

I had one request for her, "Photograph?"

She put her arm around my waist and I around her shoulders. Dema did the honor of taking the photo. With one little click of the camera lens, her image imprinted on my camera and on my heart. The photograph eventually made its way to the front of my china hutch at home in McLoud where it is a constant reminder to honor her request.

The next day, we visited a men's prison. Andrew must have dropped off Bibles during the night because they were already in the van when we boarded. While still on the bus, a large, muscular warden rehearsed basic rules with his baritone voice. We were told the bus would remain parked near the side door in case our group needed to escape quickly.

From our position on stage we watched prisoners arrive and seat themselves on hard, slatted, wooden benches. A massive drape served as the backdrop for us on an otherwise vacant stage. Alex introduced himself then continued to share the gospel message with the men. I was the last of the team to speak. As the service ended, prisoners stood and crowded the front of the auditorium, pushing and shoving their way forward en masse to get a Bible. I learned as a child to stand still when a ferocious dog approaches, never run. So I stood quietly watching the chaos just feet below where I stood, waiting for instructions from Alex or Dema, or a guard or warden, listening for a creaky side door. My eyes darted toward the side stage for any instructions. Guards restrained someone. I heard coarse shouting. A large pale prisoner with a shaved head shouted and strained to get himself loose from prison guards. He pushed his way onto the stage between a row of curtains. Alex gently pushed me behind him. "Stand right here," he said.

Dema walked toward us and told Alex the prisoner insisted on speaking to me and asked if I was willing to allow that, which I was. With Dema's assistance, the prisoner told me he was going to read his Bible and he would make sure all other prisoners read their Bibles. He wanted to make a personal promise to me he would follow through with his commitment. Then he walked shyly away, head bowed, shoulders slumped. We quickly exited through the stage side door.

The driver made a series of turns within the prison complex and stopped again before he opened the door. The prisoners wanted to show us their art. We walked a short distance to a small room where three prisoners showed us wooden boxes and trinkets they made. They were intricate and beautifully carved jewelry boxes, small and large, lined with worn pieces of red fabric. We shopped at an unofficial prison store single file. We stooped over because of the low ceiling. It was dark and damp, almost cave-like inside. When the prisoner saw interest in a product, he held it up to a tiny window where light came through. As we looked at each item, a guard entered the room carrying three small leather cases. He opened them to show us winter Russian hats, military patches, military ribbons and medals, and even knives. I bought a Russian hat, a small carved box, and a carved clock.

In the evening, we went again to the auditorium where we first met the children. We sang songs we all knew as a quartet. Some teens came on stage and sang Christian songs in Russian. Each team member greeted the small group of people and shared a little about their families and their work in the United States. Alex shared the message of salvation through Jesus Christ and invited them to receive the gift of eternal life.

With the concluding amen, people pushed toward the stage, especially teens and their mothers. Every child wanted a photograph with the team. Some mothers wanted us to help their children go to the United States. Three young teen girls Anya, Tanya, and Yulia, tried to contain younger children and put them in order for a photograph. Dema indicated it was time to leave and promised the children we would return the next morning, the last day of our stay in Orel.

The driver pulled the bus into a graveled parking lot near an open market. Russian military guards kept watch around the perimeter. Alex told us to take all the remaining Bibles and distribute them to vendors or shoppers in the market. I tried to give out the last Bible to a military guard. He waved his hand, said something in Russian, and refused it. Since I did not understand, with body language I insisted he take it. He did not. I laid it on a vendor's scarf display.

The brothel was a comfortable place after a long day. Knowing it was our last evening there, Dot and I reviewed our days in Orel until our eyes closed for the night.

With only a short time at the auditorium the next morning, we offered photo ops and talked personally with the children who understood a little English. Dema left us while he went to the train station to buy tickets for the trip back to Moscow. Time to say goodbye.

We took a city bus to the train station for an eight-hour ride to Moscow. We sat together on the bus, regretful our time in Orel was finished. Three girls carrying gifts came onto the bus refusing to leave until they spoke to us. I waved to Anya as she waited beside the bus. They brought bread and cake insisting we take it. I refused, but they persisted by placing a cake and bread in our hands with one request, "Do not forget me."

As the train rolled away from the station, Dema explained the rationed ingredients used to make the bread and cake probably represented a month of commodity distributions for the girls' families. I wept.

Their request, like that of the woman prisoner, haunted me, "Please do not forget us."

In Moscow, and one step closer to home, we relished warm showers and food. Clean comfortable presumably secure beds offered us sleep.

The day before leaving Moscow, we were invited to a Russian military base for lunch. A military general, a believer, led our small group into a large room where a long white linen cloth-covered table was set with beautiful china and stemware. Red napkins with metal rings extended a warm, formal welcome. Other uniformed Russian military officers standing behind high-backed chairs nodded their heads in greeting as we took our designated seats. The gen-

My Extraordinary Journey To The Valley Of Joy

eral sat at the head of the table. Dema sat near him to translate. Browned bread rolls lay on small white plates at each place setting. A white-clad server filled water glasses.

As waiters ladled a thin soup with bits of dark meat, carrots, cabbage, and potatoes into our shallow bowls, the general welcomed our team. I sipped liquid from the stew, then reluctantly spooned up the meat and vegetables. We ate the customary light dessert. The general assured us, as Americans and a Canadian, he planned to open the Russian military to access the gospel, assuring us every Russian soldier would receive a Bible. As the meal continued, Alex asked the general to share his own testimony of becoming a Christian. His personal journey to hearing the gospel and accepting it as truth began with a simple inspection of scripture and a quiet commitment.

In the afternoon we strolled through Red Square and the largest shopping mall in the world, where I bought another Russian clock. I had always liked clocks and hourglasses. Each tick seemed to shout, "You need to fill it with good." Sometimes I listened.

In the evening, Dema escorted us along a vacant, snow-covered street, past a well-lit Red Square where Lenin's coffin appeared as small as a twig in a forest. All the pictures

I'd seen of St Basil's colorful onion-domed center could not compare to my sense of awe of seeing it in person. I snugged my heavy coat and watched my breath cloud dissipate. Dot's voice pulled me out of the dream, calling me to catch up.

The lobby of the tall Moscow hotel was empty. Dema led us to a windowless room for a private dinner on our last night. Red-clothed tables were arranged in a square formation, leaving a vacancy in the middle. Tall-backed dark wood chairs invited us to sit.

Strangers sat at the table nearest the entry. Dema directed our team to tables near the wall away from the head table. Familiar faces smiled welcomingly at us. A week earlier, our individual teams had been sent to various cities for ministry upon arrival in Moscow. I sensed relief that we were all together again. At that moment, I realized we were really on our way home.

After everyone sat down, Dema explained that the men at the head table were eagles, pilots, and stewards, carrying Jews out of Russia and back to Israel as a fulfillment of Jeremiah 16:14-16 NIV:

"However, the days are coming," declares the LORD, "When it will no longer be said, 'As surely as the LORD

lives, who brought the Israelites up out of Egypt, but it will be said, 'As surely as the LORD lives, who brought the Israelites up out of the land of the north and out of all the countries where he had banished them. For I will restore them to the land I gave their ancestors.'

"But now I will send for many fishermen," declares the LORD, "and they will catch them. After that I will send for many hunters, and they will hunt them down on every mountain and hill and from the crevices of the rocks."

The men seated at the head table formed an under-the-radar, modern-day fishing and hunting organization, searching out and rescuing anyone who wanted to return to Israel from Russia. Hunters went into Russia to search for Jews who wanted to emigrate. At a designated time and place, pilots arrived to fly them to Israel. Those who chose to be carried on eagle's wings were allowed to take only one suitcase on a trip of no return.

Early the next morning we once again boarded an old, dented Russian plane to go to Amsterdam for an eight-hour layover. Upon arrival in Amsterdam, Alex advised us to place our carry-on luggage in a locker, so we could take a short train to downtown Amsterdam. It was a fascinating place with lots of bakeries near the town center and mimes performing on the street. Bicyclists maneuvered their way through pedestrian traffic on the plaza. Amsterdam dramatically contrasted Orel. It was my first time there, but it would not be my last.

I would not forget Amsterdam or the prisoners or the girls or the Jews returning.

Chapter 18
Pilgrimage to Israel

"I am with you and will watch over you wherever you go, and I will bring you back to this land. I will not leave you until I have done what I have promised you."
Genesis 28:15 NIV

Flying into foreign airports became routine, but this flight had its unique turbulence. Six months after my trip to Russia, Donnie and I faced challenges in another part of the world.

We walked side by side in early darkness onto the tarmac of Ben Gurion Airport in Tel Aviv. Our twelve-day tour to Israel came to an end. We went home with lots of experiential knowledge, a coffee set made in Germany, and a bottle of Yordan wine. As we approached the obviously well-used, dirty, bent-up metal, rocket-shaped plane taking us to Paris, I briefly considered asking if we could go on another flight. As I thought about it, I did what others did, kept walking in the line boarding the plane. Donnie mumbled behind me something about the appearance of the plane. I replied with an understanding nod.

Finding our seats and putting the coffee set in the overhead for safekeeping, I buckled into the middle of three seats on the pilot's side of the plane. A glum woman seated by the window peered into the darkness. Donnie sat in the aisle seat. Members of the tour group were also somber or sleepy or ready to go home. No one talked. As the plane taxied down the runway, a man in the seat across the aisle turned to Donnie and asked, "Is there supposed to be fire coming out of the engine?"

Donnie replied that it was probably the runway lights. He strained his neck to see out, unable to absolutely answer the question. The plane lifted off. As it gained altitude, my coffee set clattered from the liftoff quake. As the plane went up, the porcelain set with the pink roses shook even more. Fear of my coffee set breaking crowded any thoughts of possibly losing an engine.

Before the stewardess completed her routine safety reminders, the pilot's voice squawked through the intercom. The plane lost an engine at takeoff so he planned to dump airplane fuel in the Mediterranean Sea and return to Tel

Aviv. The window-seat lady next to me cried out, "Oh, God! Oh, God!"

I grabbed her right hand with my left. My right hand was already in Donnie's. I quoted scripture, "Though the earth be removed and the mountains be cast into the sea, I will not fear." I whispered it over and over again as the plane dumped fuel and looped back to the runway.

Donnie was stoic. I can honestly say I did not fear until I saw the ambulances, fire trucks, and emergency lights below. It occurred to me then that airport personnel believed we might crash land. After a teasing descent, the pilot roughly landed the plane to the relieved applause of passengers. We boarded another plane to Paris, with no final connections to the United States.

We survived to tell the rest of the story about our pilgrimage to Israel.

The trip to Israel was a memorable culmination of planning. Having been born in late 1948, just months after the miraculous rebirth of Israel, I became aware of significant times and seasons on God's calendar concerning the nation of Israel. Donnie's roots also tingled when he spoke of Israel as if somewhere deep in his person – there lay a buried desire to make a pilgrimage to the land. He did not like to fly, but he was willing to make a trip to Israel. Donnie's Swiss-German grandfather had been a young stowaway on a passenger ship going to America in the late 1890s. Once discovered on board by the ship's captain, Albert Kuhn played the accordion for other passengers to pay for his bed and board. Donnie's dad, Albert Jr., was Albert Kuhn Sr.'s firstborn in America. The Kuhn name is the German spelling for the Jewish name Cohen. So yes, the ancestral strings were strong.

Some friends and I attended the worship service at a Methodist church in Oklahoma City. Before the service closed, a speaker talked about taking a pilgrimage to Israel. He said a special time to go was during the Feast of Tabernacles because of the historical and spiritual significance. During the trip, we could participate in a solidarity parade sponsored by the Christian Embassy Jerusalem. I took a brochure.

Donnie was actually really excited about a trip to Israel, so we checked our finances and decided to join the tour. I wanted our sons to go, but our eldest son did not feel he could get out of college or miss his work. Our youngest son, a senior in high school, decided he wanted to stay home to work and visit friends.

The first night in Israel, we stayed in Tel Aviv in a hotel where double-glass doors provided a view of the Mediterranean Sea. I took off my shoes, raced to the seashore and plunged both sets of toes into the water. Donnie and I strolled down the beach beneath the stars like characters in a romance novel.

The second day of our tour, we made our journey to Jerusalem by bus through a gauntlet of abandoned military equipment, tanks, and trucks, all relics of the Six-Day War. We went on a historical tour, one laced with modern events of Israelis returning to the land of their ancestors.

We stayed at a Holiday Inn in Jerusalem. Although the food tasted wonderful, it was the first time Donnie had been offered fish for breakfast, which left an enduring bad taste. Being from Southwest Oklahoma, cattle and cotton country, he did not even like the smell of fish. We chose seats far from the fish bar each day for his sake.

Our tour director warned us not to eat from food carts in the Old City or at restaurants unless recommended by our guide. Donnie and I decided to eat a good breakfast, except fish, take a piece of fruit and bread for the day, then eat at the hotel in the evening. Our plan worked well. We were the only guests in our tour group who did not get ill during the trip.

The first night, we enjoyed a concert in the desert. The stars felt so close; it seemed we could touch them just by reaching toward the heavens.

Our assigned tour guide led us to several out-of-the-way places, including the old Jericho Road and the Valley of Elah, neither were included in our itinerary. From the extra excursion on the Jericho Road, I understood the song lyrics from my youth, "On the Jericho Road, there is room for just two." After our short stop in the Valley of Elah where David slew Goliath, I understood how voices could span the valley to be heard by the armies surrounding the scene of battle.

The hunters and fishers I met in Russia earlier that year had obviously been busy. Two Russian Jews manned a boat crossing the Sea of Galilee. As we returned from our excursion, I noticed a Russian flag and an Israeli flag flying side-by-side from the mast. When I asked our guide about the flags, he explained that both sailors of the vessel returned to Israel from Russia, the land of the north, in accordance with the prophet Jeremiah. I had a flashback from the last night of my trip to Russia. We tipped the Russian sailors well.

During a tour of Old City Jerusalem, our guide arranged for the group to go inside the Dome of the Rock. Enclosed there was the piece of granite where tradition marks as the place where Abraham offered his son Isaac as a sacrifice to God. But, God provided a ram for a sacrifice in Isaac's place. We held hands and prayed silently.

The Dead Sea became a living experience for Donnie and me as we floated on the briny liquid. Our skin stung with the mineral-dense bath. We stayed long enough for the experience and fled to showers of freshwater along the shore where we rinsed off the deadness.

After leaving the salty seaside, our group left for a short trip to Masada where our tour guide shared a history lesson from the place where the Roman Army fought against the last Jewish stronghold before the Jewish temple was destroyed. During our stay in Israel we visited kibbutzes, small, communal farms, where we learned about the unique farming methods being used to literally make the desert bloom, an ancient prophecy foretold of it.

We planted a tree in honor of Donnie's family.

We walked the streets of Jerusalem where youths threw dirty water at us. Our tour director told us to stay together when in the Old City because a man had been stabbed from behind.

Our bus could not go to Rachel's tomb because of a bomb threat, but we could visit Bethlehem.

At the Wailing Wall, we were allowed to write one prayer request on a piece of tiny paper, fold it and place it in a mortar space in the wall. Donnie let me have both request pieces. Both were answered, not immediately, but in God's time.

A parade the following day welcomed the beginning of The Feast of Tabernacles. Donnie and I wore our specially-made shirts as we marched with others to show our solidarity for the nation. As we walked and sang and danced through the streets during the Feast, our route passed high-rise apartments with cloth booths draped over patios in commemoration of the Jewish feast commanded by God through Moses. After the parade, Prime Minister Yitzak Rabin spoke at an assembly at the Christian Embassy Jerusalem. The trip was far too short to experience all we wanted of this ancient land. We packed the last day not knowing what lay ahead.

A new connection in Paris kept us flying forward to home. We survived.

Chapter 19
Hungary in November 1995

"Then you will call upon me and come and pray to me, and I will listen to you. You will seek me and find me when you seek me with all your heart." Jeremiah 29: 12-13 NIV

While I worked at Life Christian Center as an administrative assistant after a break from the newspaper, I heard the familiar name of Glen Howard, a missionary I remembered from my teen years. His ancestors had once pastored the Pentecostal Holiness Church in McLoud. Glen came to visit the pastor a few times while I worked there. He did not recognize me, but I read up on his current work and learned he served in Hungary. One day, I asked about his work. He invited me to come to Hungary and see what God was doing.

Despite the cold Hungarian weather in November, my brother and sister-in-law, George and Shirley Palmer, agreed to accompany me. Glen made arrangements to pick us up at the airport. Glen offered a cozy, comfortable apartment during our time in Budapest.

Glen assigned a young Ethiopian woman named Missy to assist us with translation and touring Budapest. She took us sightseeing in the Old Town area. We enjoyed a short train ride on our own to Szentendre, Hungary, where we visited the city and ate lunch.

Glen and Ellen considered coming back to the States in a few years, leaving the International Church of Budapest in the hands of those he prepared for leadership. He explained that missionaries and pastors should always be training the next generation to take leadership. This was necessary because open doors can often close and one must always remember their work is temporary in this life. The Howards developed a Bible curriculum that could be mailed all over Europe, so their legacy lasted long after their season in Hungary ended. It became apparent to me while listening to Glen's plan that a church should be an organism growing in many directions from the center. I concluded that God never meant for the Church to be cloistered behind doors or encompassed by walls but should be in constant motion and expansion. Every healthy cell within the local church has a place to be, a reason to be, and people to serve, past the doors, outside the walls.

The church service we attended at the International Church of Budapest was special for me. They offered two options for taking communion: to take it from a common cup or to take it individually. I could also choose between real wine and grape juice. It wasn't about the symbols themselves, but the blood and body of Christ being remembered as the Lord commanded. Glen presented us with honorary memberships to the International Church of Budapest. I was already a member of the body of Christ, but the certificate was a nice confirmation of common faith.

While we were in Hungary, Glen told us how he had pulled away from the denomination that sent him to Europe because denominations were divisive. As a unity of faith, he had visited other Christian churches in Budapest and paid a tithe to some of them in an act of unification. The Apostle Paul wrote there should be no divisions in the body of Christ. This was the first time I had seen that put into action. I was determined to never allow denominational lines to separate me from my brothers and sisters in Christ Jesus.

The last evening of our stay, Glen took us to see an old castle near the Danube. Street lights cast an eerie spell over the whole scene. While George and Shirley toured the castle, Glen and I stood outside. We watched people with muffs on their hands and furry hats on their heads skate in circles on the ice-covered river. The scene looked like a moving image of a Norman Rockwell Christmas card. I walked away from Glen. Standing beneath heavy evergreens, when I sensed the Spirit nudge me. I spied out the land but found no giants for me to conquer in post-World War II Budapest. The International Church in Budapest expanded like a light in the darkness. I did not work in Hungary on a regular basis, but I took what I learned to a different place at a different time, in God's time.

I held in survival mode until God nudged me again.

Chapter 20
Between the Time and Lines

"Son of man, I have made you a watchman for the house of Israel; so hear the word I speak and give them warning from me." Ezekiel 33: 7 NIV

Being a soccer mom and taking the boys to Cub Scouts faded to memories. Donnie's son was already grown. The two young men in our home were learning to drive and earning funds to support this new skill.

Gary graduated high school in 1990 and worked his way through college. He struggled with combining work and study and driving home to McLoud every day.

Steady Donnie continued to work at Tinker Air Force Base. We constructed McLoud Self-Storage in the spring of 1994, expanding it in 1996. I managed the business and together we also bought several houses for rentals. I literally found myself scrubbing bathrooms with toothbrushes in some of those rentals.

After two-and-a-half years at Life Christian Center School, Gregory wanted to return to McLoud High School to graduate with his class. I sensed my time as an administrative assistant to the pastor was over, and I should go back to McLoud to manage our businesses. I bloomed best where God planted me: McLoud. I crossed a bridge and sensed a new season emerging.

While working at the church part-time for three years, I completed a by-the-mail course in writing for children. I also earned my ministerial license through Life Christian Center. My ordination as a Bible teacher in 1994 frightened me because of the weight of responsibility. Ezekiel 33: 1-7 was the text used during the ordination ceremony.

Ezekiel 33: 1-7 NIV, "The word of the LORD came to me: Son of man, speak to your countrymen and say to them: 'When I bring the sword against a land, and the people of the land choose one of their men and make him their watchman, and he sees the sword coming against the land and blows the trumpet to warn the people, then if anyone hears the trumpet but does not take warning, and the sword comes and takes his life, his blood will be on his own head. Since he heard the sound of the trumpet but did not take warning his blood will be on his own head. If he had taken warning, he would've saved himself. But if the watchman sees the sword coming and does not blow the trumpet to warn the people and the sword comes and takes the life of one of them, that man will be taken away because of his sin, but I will hold the watchman accountable for his blood.'

'Son of man, I have made you a watchman for the house of Israel; so hear the word I speak and give them warning from me.'"

Taking responsibility for others was not a new commission. When Mama went to work in Oklahoma City, she held me responsible for everything that happened in the house while she was away at work. It did not matter who left the dirty dishes on the coffee table or refused to clean a bedroom, I was responsible. Of course, I held no real authority to make anyone do chores or let me know where they were going or when they would be home.

Despite my troublesome encounter with taking responsibility for others, I accepted the commission in my heart, pondering and praying, sleeping and eating, doing what humans do, living each filled day, yet always sensing a certain amount of responsibility to help right wrongs where I could.

Most of what I earned financially during my tenure at Life Christian Center paid tuition for Gregory to attend school. Now that he returned to public school, financially I needed to find a full-time job, but I wanted to write. I longed to be in full-time Christian ministry. Searching for God's plan seemed much like finding the best paprika among the thousands to taste in Hungary: lots of colorful options, but no way to know whether cool taste or fire lies within each decision.

While I worked at the church part-time, I wrote for others. I wrote several manuscripts and listened to a lot of stories from those who thought they wanted to write a book. I hired one of the students at Life Christian Center School to illustrate a children's book for me. She was thrilled to be a paid artist. I worked my way through a self-publishing path and released my first children's book, *Let's Be Friends - a Jungle Legend.*

My confidence was bolstered by the publication of the book. Now I wanted to write about my home town, so I visited an elderly friend, Mattie Petricek, after work on Thursdays. Mattie's parents arrived in the McLoud area shortly after the Kickapoo Land Run in 1895. She told me stories from her life, some of the same stories each week, adding little details as she remembered them. I took notes.

When I had collected all her stories, I asked her permission to compile them in a book. She was elated. When I finished writing, I read the stories to her and she gave me a little clarification as needed. Newspaper sports photographer Rick Sanders who worked with me in the past photographed a rosebud he used for a beautiful cover design. When it was complete, I was ready to self-publish *Mattie - In Search of God*.

A crossroad loomed, and I could see a fork in my journey. I needed a paying job. I tried to make it selling real estate, but the market was down in the late 1990s. Our self-storage business would not be profitable for a few years. I longed to work for the newspaper again, perhaps to write something more people wanted to read or to resurrect the happy years or to serve my community. I wasn't even sure I could make a salary from it, but my McLoud roots tingled too much to be anywhere else.

My three-year non-compete clause from the sale of the newspaper in 1991 had run its course, so with the help of family friend Rick Sanders, I decided to open a second newspaper in McLoud. My mother offered to invest ten thousand dollars if I established a startup paper. It was 1996, thirty years after she told me never to ask her for anything.

I never asked. Mama and I had both healed through the years.

Rick set up the computers and named the publication. He designed the mast and layout. With Mom's loan, I also bought a printer, incorporated the paper, and went to work urging advertisers that the *Regional Community Register* was a good weekly tabloid. We covered news in McLoud, Dale, and Newalla.

I was truly back home. Donnie and I attended the McLoud First Assembly of God Church again under a new pastor, and I taught a young adult Sunday school class, expanding my small-town roots into another generation, growing deeper in local soil. The *Regional Community Register* made a profit from the start, even with loan payback. With the storage business and now the newspaper, it seemed like we were heading into a season of new beginnings.

Chapter 21
Selling Out

"It is the character of water to move in outward ripples when a pebble is thrown into it. It is the character of mankind to move beyond themselves and affect others. Their decisions have a ripple effect. A wise man will consider this before making a decision." Glenda Kuhn

One day a man walked into the *Regional Community Register* newspaper office introducing himself as a representative from Dominion Corporation. He was asking if I knew anyone who was interested in selling land west of McLoud. He explained he was searching for land for the construction of a proposed women's prison. I named off a couple of possible sellers. Because I held a real estate license, I kept up on what was selling and who was buying in the area. After he left the office with a list of landowners I knew west of town, I phoned Mama. She owned over one-hundred acres. She lived alone on the farm after my stepdad's death. I believed she did not have any intention of selling, but if a neighbor said they sold their land for a good price, she would complain that she wished she had known.

To my surprise, Mama was interested in selling her land. She feared being shot by neighbors who were shooting her cattle. Another piece of land located south of her farm sold to a developer. When he cut roads into his new addition, mud washed into one of her ponds, filling it half up in one rainy season.

She sold the land to Dominion Corporation for use as a private women's prison for non-maximum-security prisoners. McLoud residents protested the project. Even though McLoud couldn't boast a new industry for more than thirty years, some people opposed the human industry. After my mother sold the farm, she built a new home in town. The prison later sold to the State of Oklahoma and became Mable Bassett Correctional Center, which included maximum security prisoners.

I sold the *Regional Community Register* the next year after Mama sold her land for the prison. A larger firm bought both newspapers in McLoud and sold them to a regional group of family newspapers. It would be several years before McLoud had another newspaper.

Was opening another newspaper a good decision? Only God knows. After all, He was there with me in and through it. I finished my season writing news and hoped to apply my craft in other directions.

After selling the newspaper, I felt how I once saw an old, mother dog act as she nursed eight puppies. When the babies finally slept, she was too tired to get up to replenish her strength. I was just as empty.

As an introvert, quiet times were precious and I experienced limited numbers of those for as long as I could remember. I scattered prayers with little focus on answers. Sleep was never restful. Focusing on any task proved laborious. My husband felt like a stranger because we never shared meaningful conversations. I ate little, but gained weight due to hypothyroidism. My strength was drained, spirit, soul and body.

My time in the newspaper was complete. My fourth-grade dream of writing news had ended.

Chapter 22
Ukrainian Winters

"For this is what the LORD, the God of Israel, says: 'The jar of flour will not be used up and the jug of oil will not run dry...'" I Kings 17:14, NIV

The air was cold even when the sun shone through puffs of bright white cotton clouds in Korosten, Ukraine, in November 1998. I walked on several inches of soiled, scarred, packed ice. Looking across a field, I saw the tops of weeds sticking through the snow, weeds that clearly had not been mowed the summer before and must now be head high. All the nuclear-infused water was cold, even water used for bathing. Only bottled water was drinkable since the Chernobyl nuclear accident of 1986 and the aging lead pipes further contaminated every drop.

Alex of the Russian team asked me to form a second smaller team to help distribute Christmas gifts to orphans and youth within a fifty-mile circle from the ghostly, vacated city of Chernobyl. He ministered through Freedom

Village Ukraine, a humanitarian aid organization based in New York. Thousands of children continued to live with disabilities and the effects of radiation after Chernobyl. All around Ukraine, the side effects of radiation impacted an entire generation. Ukraine reeled in the wake of economic depression from the financial collapse of the Soviet Union. I sensed God inviting me to go to Ukraine. Jesus Christ sent out His disciples in pairs, so I asked others to go with me.

A plane carrying the McLoud First Assembly of God group arrived in Kiev to bitter vast, open, snow-covered fields. Alex met our small team of three -- Susan, Vicki, and myself -- at the airport. We maximized luggage size and weight to take what we needed plus gifts for Freedom Village children in the area. We filled our checked luggage with gifts made by women prisoners from Central Oklahoma Correctional Center, later Mabel Bassett prison, near McLoud where I volunteered in a quilting craft class. The prisoners made afghans, quilts, and stuffed toys. How we would pass them out, I did not know, but they were made by women who empathetically shared the pain of confinement to a system and isolation from children who needed someone to comfort them.

Our team of three women joined together to travel to Ukraine to deliver gifts and give out lots of loving hugs. Leading Susan and Vicki on their first missionary journey made me feel like I introduced two young Oklahoma women to a vast world outside their small towns. Susan was just a child when John Cuzick pastored the McLoud First Assembly of God and I taught Sunday school. Now, we were experiencing a first for both of us with this mission trip to Ukraine. Vicki, a vibrant and talented mother of two young children, enthusiastically wanted to broaden her experiences. She worked with children at the church in McLoud. I knew the trip could transform each young woman. I did not realize how it would transform me as well.

The McLoud team, which joined others in Kiev, boarded a bus for a nighttime drive through forest and glen, past moments of lights from small convenience stores called magazines through tiny dark villages to Korosten, Ukraine. Korosten was not well-lit either, and the bus pulled up to a large four-story building. Carrying overfilled suitcases, Alex led team members through large doors and made a sharp right turn. Noises came from a stairwell. Suddenly, a group of teenagers with wide smiles appeared. Some were obviously challenged physically or mentally. They grabbed handles on suitcases saying, "Big hello," a welcoming committee I'd never experienced. As I started up the stairs, a young man with one leg tucked beneath him plunked his slightly heavy torso on the next step.

"Hi, I am Igor. I am your translator," he announced.

Igor ignored my pleading that it was too heavy for him to tug upstairs and grabbed my suitcase, pulling it behind him one stair at a time. His friend Victor grabbed the other suitcase and sprinted to the top.

Smells of stew and bread greeted my olfactory nerves. A cook and her son prepared a daily menu for us for the next eight days: soup with potatoes, carrots, onions, and sometimes a little meat. Some team members said it was horse meat because of its dark color, just as we suspected in Russia. Sometimes we ate bread too because a bakery behind the building provided fresh bread daily. Residents of Freedom Village Ukraine worked at the bakery. In the morning, we ate chicken soup with potatoes, carrots, onions, and bread with jam. We drank instant coffee or one cup of slightly warm tea. We each brought our own supplemental foods in case we could not tolerate what was being served.

Susan lived on the instant oatmeal she packed at home because her stomach did not adjust to the food change. We used bottled water, even for brushing our teeth.

Team members shared small rooms with two or three beds and a nightstand as well as a common restroom down the hall. Radiators exuded warmth when they could. Flannel pajamas never felt so good. Showers were cold. It was impossible to wear enough layers to be cozy. Nothing warm seemed to exist, inside the building or out.

Freedom Village shipped Christmas gifts. Each morning young men from the building loaded the gifts onto a bus. Teams boarded the bus and went to the orphanage of the day. Usually, Igor and Victor serenaded us along the way. Victor liked to sing "We shall see the King" in English.

As we became acquainted with teens living at Freedom Village Ukraine, we learned each person's tragic story. The parents of some could not provide for them, but many were totally abandoned. After returning from Christmas deliveries each day, we spent evenings playing games and talking with young people living on the bottom two floors. Poor, elderly people lived on the two top floors.

One morning, the bus rolled out of Freedom Village for the tiny village of Radomyshl. After passing many miles of rich plowed farmland peeking from beneath the snow, the bus driver stopped in front of a long, low, wood-sided building. Pigs grunted beneath a battered barn near what looked like a long dormitory, creating a backdrop for the small crosses and large stones of a make-shift cemetery enclosed by a short metal fence.

A woman who served as janitor and cook pulled snow aside to expose several fresh, crossless mounds. Our translator explained the orphans of Radomyshl were buried in the small cemetery. Managers of the school, a man and woman, ushered team members into what could have been an office, only because it had a desk and chair. After translated introductions and instructions for meeting the children, we began our guided tour through shotgun rooms filled with small children segregated according to the severity of their disabilities. Wood smoke mingled with the smell of urine filled our nostrils.

The administrator told us the children were not neglected but must sit only on floors or benches built along the walls due to the extreme disabilities, but we were still shocked at what we saw. Scenes unfolding along our stroll through dark rooms with only one small window open to ventilate the wood-stoked heaters, caused us to squint from the light of the window to see the almost naked bodies of children lying on the benches and seated on the dirt floor. Groans emanated from places deep within the souls of children. Some could only toss on their beds or on the floor. Their rocking bodies seated on legless benches attached to the wall swayed in a rhythm only they could hear. Cold rooms sectioned off into ten-foot squares were dark and damp from humidity and urine. Before coming, we filled our pockets with candies to give to the children, but the administrator instructed us not to pass out treats because they would eat them quickly, wrappers and all.

We could give them nothing but compassionate looks, touches, and blankets. We left cans of meat, beans, rice, dry milk, and other non-perishables, along with the candy in our pockets with the administrators to distribute as they desired. The children did not own toys or teddy bears, nothing for comfort, except the small blankets we brought. Obviously malnourished, bony bodies were covered mostly in light cotton shrouds with their shaved heads poking through the neckline. I felt as if the children were rocking themselves into an eternal sleep, waiting for the final moment.

Higher-functioning children in one room owned some toys brought on previous trips by Freedom Village Ukraine, so we left a few to replace the broken pieces around the room. Some of the children tried to communicate, taking our hands, patting our coats, pulling our hands to their faces, rubbing them on their cheeks.

As we somberly stepped onto the bus, I offered the bus driver a nutrition bar. Turning it over and over in his hand, he returned it. After everyone loaded the bus, Alex whispered that some Ukrainians believed Americans brought poison or outdated food to give them, which explained why the driver refused my offer.

The Freedom Village team visited a day school for the disabled near Korosten. The loose windows let in the cold and the rugs thrown about on the concrete floor did little to block the dampness penetrating it. Everyone wore a sweater or coat inside the building. I was becoming accustomed to living in my coat. Cooks and teachers were kind, asking often through a translator for supplies for the children. Parents begged us to help them for their child's sake.

Teachers at the day school taught students at their own level. Those who could joined together to enact dramatic scenes. The joy of every performer is a wider, more diverse audience. Broad smiles split faces as students who were able performed a Christmas drama complete with colorful costumes. The school director served the team sweets and drinks, a small reception hosted by teachers and parents.

After breakfast the following morning, team members once again boarded a bus. Joined by other team members and Freedom Village residents, Alex assigned us to passing out Christmas gifts to children and directors. Landscapes all looked the same, except bright sunshine illuminated the day. Once again, Victor and Igor sang as bus passengers lumbered past empty ice-packed fields where dried grass sticks poked their stems from beneath to wave a frigid hello. A heavy-coat-clad, burly driver kept his gaze ahead without acknowledging the people who surrounded him. The only expression I saw from his face was when he moved his heavy mustache from side to side as he maneuvered the vehicle around potholes. He pulled the bus to a stop in front of a large multi-storied building in the countryside, and opened the door. Children from Freedom Village had already loaded containers of Christmas gifts in the back of the bus. As we unloaded the gifts, Alex encouraged each of us to be prepared to share something about our faith.

The auditorium smelled of chalk and sweaty bodies. High ceilings, concrete walls, and ornate tiled floors amplified the voices and footsteps of many children. Teachers attempted to calm the children's excitement without any success.

After the program, which many could not hear above the roar of the children's chatter, and the presentation of gifts to teachers and administrators, we distributed gifts to the children. It struck me as odd that we gave more gifts to the administrators than to the children. Alex explained employees received more gifts first because they received no salary for their work at the orphanage. Workers were tempted to take donations given to the orphans to use for their own families, so Freedom Village hoped by giving them more, they would take less from the children. We left all food and hygiene products with the administrators. In addition to the distributed gifts and treats, Freedom Village also shipped in bags of flour, powdered milk, canned meats, and other commodities which both employees and children could enjoy.

Administrators in the large orphanage wanted us to tour the school. Young women learned to sew in a separate building with sewing machines. Boys, in another outbuilding, learned wood working with equipment furnished by Freedom Village Ukraine. The orphanage didn't employ craft teachers, but it was good to know they intended to formally train them when teachers could be found.

When we returned to the bus, Igor talked excitedly with the bus driver. Something changed. The driver smiled broadly as we climbed aboard. He nodded his head to each person as they boarded. Igor shared that he led the bus driver to a personal relationship with Jesus Christ while we distributed gifts in the orphanage.

Freedom Village in Korosten did not own a television; in fact, there were no electronics of any kind except a phone on the hall wall near the kitchen door. Residents made their own entertainment. One evening, students at Freedom Village filled two-liter soda bottles with candy from the abundance sent from the United States. There was plenty of Good & Plenty, so they weighted ten bottles with the little candy pellets. Setting them up at the end of the hallway like bowling pins then used a ball to roll into them. It made for a hilarious game of good and plenty bowling.

One afternoon, we went shopping for gifts for family and friends back home. Alex took us to the market, the cold outdoor arena where heavy, wool hats and coats were enticing but too bulky for return luggage. We haggled for prices on a few small items for our families, but our guide encouraged us to wait for a different shopping opportunity.

After leaving the market, Alex took us to a porcelain factory. Women stood along the sidewalk shrouded in bulky woolen overcoats, heads topped with bright print scarves or fur hats, offering to sell beautiful tea sets, bowls, and a sundry of ceramic wares. Alex explained he sent a message to announce we were coming, so they stood in the cold hoping to sell something to the Americans. It might be their only income that day, maybe for a week, or the month. I didn't dare haggle, but paid the equivalent of about five dollars each for two beautiful tea sets and let them keep the change.

On Sunday we attended a small church in Korosten. I noticed the pastor was missing the middle finger on each hand. Communists cut off his fingers to try to get him to divulge names of believers in the underground church. He served time in a Russian prison because of his faith but quickly returned to preaching after he was freed.

Before going to Ukraine, I wrote a letter to Anya and Tanya, the girls in Russia who asked me not to forget them. Yulia moved to another city shortly after the Russia trip. Anya and Tanya did not know where she was living, but I had not forgotten her. One night, Igor came to my room to tell me the Russian girls phoned him from the train station, asking for me. Anya and Tanya rode a train eighteen hours from Orel, Russia to see me in Ukraine. I was thrilled. Thankfully, Freedom Village had a room for them, and Igor made a great translator. We gave them gifts and food and a few extra dollars to take home. The bus dropped them off at a train station near the largest McDonald's restaurant in the world in Kiev as we went to the airport.

I returned to Ukraine in November 1999. This time my brother George and his wife, Shirley, joined me, along with a young woman J. M.. I contacted our friends from Russia to let them know our plans. Anya and Tanya made the eighteen-hour train ride to Ukraine again to see us.

Women from the First Assembly of God Church in McLoud made fifty plush dolls for the most physically challenged children of Radomyshl who could not own toys with buttons or strings. We used a pattern to cut gingerbread-men from muslin and painted on faces and clothing. Women prisoners from Central Oklahoma Correctional Center where I volunteered crocheted blankets and toys for the team to carry to Ukraine.

Igor met me again and immediately helped with luggage and asked to meet the other members of our team. His English improved from using it with so many ministry groups.

Igor again assigned himself to serve as our friend and personal translator. He and his friend Victor agreed to entertain us on our visits through the valleys and dales of northern Ukraine.

The first day we left Korosten to visit orphanages, J. M. and I dressed as clowns. We heard voices calling from open windows on the top two floors. The elders were calling to us, "Claus, claus," Ukrainian for clowns. We waved and decided to wear our clown suits when we visited them, if our request to do so was approved.

George, Shirley, and I sang our Ukrainian children's song at each site. What we lacked in pronunciation, they seemed to appreciate in our sincere attempt. We sang to them. They sang to us. We arrived in their world and they wanted to give back to us.

But the day we were scheduled to go to Radomyshl, Alex suggested we go without the clown suits because clown faces might frighten the children. From the bus window, I noticed the number of crosses in the small cemetery had multiplied. A few unmarked mounds of newly-turned soil indicated the numbers of deaths were still growing.

Administrators at Radomyshl wanted to meet in the office as before, welcoming us with drinks and snacks. They requested we leave all treats and toys in the office to be distributed at their discretion. Freedom Village leaders gave the administrator a financial gift before we were allowed to visit the children. It wasn't a bribe, but without it, the visits would be denied.

I asked if we could personally present the dolls to the severely challenged children because I wanted to get photos of them with the dolls to take home to the ladies who made them. No doubt the financial gift softened the administrator a bit, and they allowed us to go into the small dark rooms where the children were confined. I placed a soft doll in a little girl's hand for a photo op. She hugged the doll so strongly, it looked like a squished biscuit roll with head and legs. Immediately, other children noticed and tried to take it away from her. We distributed dolls to all who wanted one. There were just enough dolls for each child at Radomyshl, exactly enough.

One evening, J.M. and I dressed in clown garb and visited a small children's hospital not far from Freedom Village. Doctors earned the equivalent of thirty dollars a month. The hospital didn't serve meals; instead, families brought food for family members who were in the hospital. Patients weren't given medicine because there was none to give. With Igor's assistance, we distributed candies to children who could eat them and gave out small gifts with permission.

On my previous trip, I learned two facts: the elderly lived in the top floors of the building at Freedom Village in Korosten and hardly anyone in Ukraine owned mirrors. In light of those facts, we limited our clothing so we could fill our luggage with Avon cologne samples, combs, and small mirrors as gifts for them.

With some persuasion from the Freedom Village Ukraine administrator, the director of the elder apartments allowed the clowns and friends to visit the residents. Not knowing how many residents lived in the rooms, J.M. and I filled a sack and my clown suit pockets with everything I brought. The upstairs residents answered the door with joy at the sight of the clowns. Our real smiles were almost as big as the painted smiles of our costumes. The women opened the cologne sachets with a sniff and smile. They hugged the mirrors to their breasts. An elderly couple shared one apartment. She opened the sachets and smiled teasingly at her husband. He combed his hair and returned the flirt.

Language is not always verbal. Like mispronounced words, body language can be easily misunderstood. One lady wanted to dance as her gift to us. I had a great time as I danced with her in my clown suit. Then the administrator told me the lady thought I might be making fun of her. Of course, I stopped and simply clapped to the fast beat of her feet.

Some of the men opened their doors with military sternness. One even asked to see our papers. Even the gift of a comb did not deter his demands, but he took the comb while continuing to mumble his commands. Others seemed to soften when they saw we offered a gift.

Accompanied by an administrator, J.M. and I continued going door to door throughout the facility. As we came to the last apartment, I did not have anything left. My bag was empty. My pockets were empty. I asked J.M. if she had any more items to give. No! As the door opened, I once again put my hand in a pocket I had already checked. Another sachet! One more mirror.

When our small, happy group returned to the facility office, the translator asked me if I had a gift for the nurse and administrator because custom dictated giving a gift to them. I did not have anything left. My mind rehearsed if I could give them anything in our room. Since it was near the end of our stay, even my luggage was empty.

"Check and see," said the embarrassed translator. "We must give them something."

I put my hands in a front pocket and found sachets. I handed them to the administrator with a smile, but there were none for the nurse.

I began to poke my hands in all the pockets of the overalls I wore with the clown suit. There, in one of the lower pockets, I found sachets and a comb. I handed the nurse her small gift.

Like the oil that never ran dry, God provided just enough.

I have not returned to Ukraine, but Ukraine came to me. Igor came to McLoud a few years after Freedom Village closed to tell his story to our church and others. During the years after that visit, Igor used his talents to visit, by phone or in-person, many physically and mentally challenged adults and children who were confined to apartments or homes. He taught them about Jesus while caring for them personally.

Ten years after his first visit, Igor came to McLoud again. He was coordinating summer camps for handicapped people of all ages and their caregivers with the help of Ukrainian churches and friends from abroad. When he visited America, a church from Tecumseh, Oklahoma, pastored by Dennis and Willene Stone, adopted his ministry of hosting summer camps for the physically and mentally challenged.

Igor envisioned renting a complex where people with disabilities and their caregivers could get out of their homes and come together with people who shared similar life challenges. During the week-long camps, Igor and his friends taught age-appropriate Bible studies, played games, shared music, and their personal stories. Each attendee and leader left happier and healthier than when they came. Reports of renewed hope for life abounded from those who attended. Even more so, the caregivers reported great relief to know they were not alone.

Doctors performed surgery on Igor's stump of leg so he could be fitted with an appliance to hold his weight while he walked. He later moved back to his home village. He married Lesya who assists him in ministry to the physically and mentally challenged. Igor and Lesya also continue to train up disciples in the small village church where he grew up

Chapter 23
Bulgaria

"Still other seed fell on good soil where it produced a crop - a hundred, sixty or thirty times what was sown."
Matthew 13:8 NIV

Part of my work at Life Christian Center involved researching Christian current events and trends for the pastor by reading Christian magazines and newsletters. On one of these magazine research assignments, I noticed a small one-inch ad for a group called Turkish World Outreach. Because of my earlier vision of a man sitting on a hillside praying someone would tell him about Jesus, I was interested in how they were serving Turkey while living in the United States. I wrote a personal letter to Turkish World Outreach asking about their ministry. They responded to my request with brochures and a history of their organization.

One of the ways Turkish World Outreach contacted people in Turkey was by sending out gospel tracts translated in their language, compiling addresses from phone books.

Each month, volunteers received ten gospel tracts and a set of addresses. The only cost to the volunteer was an overseas stamp and envelopes. It sounded easy, so I sent tracts. If someone responded to Turkish World Outreach, the organization sent them Bible study materials and contacts to house churches. If I received a personal contact from the letters I sent, I forwarded it to the main office in Grand Junction, Colorado. Staff in Grand Junction translated the letters and responded to the recipient and also the volunteer in the United States.

Several years after I began sending Christian tracts to Turkey, I received a letter from a Turkish-speaking pastor in Bulgaria. I forwarded it to the Grand Junction office. A few weeks later I received a letter telling me the pastor asked for Christian materials and humanitarian aid for his small congregation. Turkish World Outreach suggested I find a Sunday school class or group to help the Bulgarian pastor.

I put the letter in my Bible to pray for the pastor and the situation. However, I did not want to send money to people I did not know. When I do not know what to do, I wait and pray.

Donnie and I liked to walk in the evenings. Sometimes we stopped at my older brother's house for a little conversation about missions. One evening, my brother George suggested combining our prayers and setting up an organization for God to open doors to minister to people where no one else served. I agreed with George but had no concept of where such a step into ministry would lead. Reminiscent of the song we often sang when missionaries visited the McLoud Pentecostal Holiness Church, "I'll go where you want me to go, dear Lord," my heart pulled me into agreement with George. With Shirley and Donnie at our sides, we stepped out.

George chose the name Grace Missionary Society. He filled out all the necessary forms for becoming a faith-based, non-profit organization, we were ready to serve through this uniquely-formed ministry. We agreed that no officers or members would receive salaries or reimbursement for travel. All funds donated through Grace would go toward the designated program. Grace would not take photos for promotion or do fundraising for the ministry. General funds would be distributed through an agreement of officers: George as secretary/treasurer, Shirley as president, and me as director of missions. Donnie agreed to become a helper in all Grace chose to do, as long as he was not asked to preach, teach or sing.

As an organization, we determined the ministry would be faithful, not necessarily large, but faithful to the task. We agreed not to do any fundraising.

A community food pantry opened in McLoud, but when their sponsor withdrew, they were going to be forced to rent a building. Without a sponsoring organization, there would be no one to pay rent. Grace Missionary Society agreed to pay the rent for an old building in downtown McLoud.

One evening as Donnie and I walked, we again stopped by George and Shirley's house. As we discussed missions, George said he always believed God would send him to Bulgaria.

"I know a guy in Bulgaria!" I exclaimed. "I will get the envelope and bring it to you."

I gave George the envelope and letter sent to me by a pastor requesting assistance in Bulgaria. George reached out to the man on the envelope, Rumen B. from Sliven, Bulgaria. Following the example of Joshua and Caleb spying out the land to determine if giants infested it, George and his son, Nathan, traveled to Bulgaria in April 2000.

Pastor Rumen asked a Bulgarian Christian friend, Stoyan (Tony, as he wanted to be known), to take him to Sofia to retrieve George and Nathan from the airport. Upon arrival in Nadezhda, George reported Nadezhda was definitely the darkest place he ever visited. Electricity was on-again, off-again in the metal wall enclosed district with about twenty-five thousand residents. Two public water spouts furnished water for thousands of people. Few had water faucets in their homes. Some residents heated the water on a one-burner electric appliance so it could be used for cooking and bathing. People went to the restroom wherever they found a spot. Pastor Rumen and his family used a hole in the floor with a sheer curtain hung over it in a feeble attempt at privacy. Hepatitis hovered around every corner and on every surface waiting for a host.

The giants in Bulgaria were hunger, thirst, ignorance, and self-serving traditions lurking among the hopeless in the district named Nadezhda, which ironically meant hope. George and Nathan reported little hope within the tall rusty metal plank walls confining its residents within a few ragged square miles.

Nadezhda was located across the railroad tracks from the main Bulgarian populations in the eighth-largest city in

Bulgaria, Sliven. Under Communism, the people who lived in Nadezhda, mostly Roma and Turks, earned some income because the government assigned all people a task. After the Soviet Union was dismantled, there were no jobs, therefore no source of income for Nadezhda residents who lived crammed into makeshift shelters. The people were uneducated and poor, with an average lifespan of forty-five years old.

A Bulgarian teacher led a segregated public school for the Turks and Roma residents of Nadezhda just outside the walls of the neighborhood, but this proved a fruitless venture as the teacher could not communicate with the students.

Residents of Nadezhda financially depended on charity, musician work, farm work, and dumpster diving for resale items. Farmers hired residents to work the fields in the harvest season, but the farmworkers complained the farmers did not pay them for their labor. Children carried a bucket or plastic sack searching dumpsters for morsels of food. Adults crossed the railroad tracks, passing beyond the metal fence, to dumpster dive in that more prosperous area of Sliven.

Rumen B., the pastor who made the plea through Turkish World Outreach, told George and Nathan many evangelists visited Nadezhda, took photos of the people, and left some money. None returned. He believed photos taken during these visits were used to get contributions for the organization, but the people did not get any of it. George and Nathan saw signs for Christian churches within the walls of the ghetto, but they were closed. We would later learn most Christian ventures lasted less than three months.

Old traditions confined the people in Nadezhda even more than their economic circumstances. Their own life patterns cast them to a set of social rules through which they could not thrive. They believed education wasted time when a child could be more useful in the vineyards or dumpster diving, so illiteracy reigned. Girls were expected to marry once they began their menses, often as young as twelve. Boys were expected to marry their assigned bride by about sixteen. Young couples lived with their parents, who often lived with grandparents. Women bore children when they were but children themselves. A cycle of dysfunction reigned.

Roma were known for their sorcery. Taking advantage of *gadje*, non-Gypsies, was not only expected but celebrated if money changed hands in exchange for predictions. Custom dictated a social order within the walls. Turks segregated themselves from the ethnic Roma. Roma separated themselves from the "naked" Roma, those without homes, clothes, or employment.

A horse was the status symbol for the Roma. Those with a horse and wagon could travel along highways to reach further out from their central residence to find work or haul wood for heating. The wheels of the Gypsy carts turned in Nadezhda, but without measurable fruitful motion, spirit, soul, or body. Generations followed the other with minimal change.

The Spirit of the Lord led George and Nathan to meet another man in Sliven, a young English teacher named Danail. Nathan made quick friends with Danail, offering to pay him to teach English to the young Christian men of Nadezhda so they could become employed. Nathan, through Grace Missionary Society, paid for five of those young men to get a driver's license. With a little knowledge of the English language and a driver's license, each found employment, thus sprouting a seed of new hope for the youth of Nadezhda.

I first traveled to Nadezhda in November 2000. As I prayerfully walked through the streets and met the people, I knew I landed where I would plant my heart. In the early years, we made quick trips to assess needs and make plans, usually eight days at the longest. George said we should get in the country and back out before our presence was detected.

George's warning proved right. At the end of that first trip on the last evening as we worshipped with believers in Nadezhda, a group of men in white shirts and black slacks arrived in black cars. Barging through the door to the small half-basement building, some of the men in the room spoke loudly to them. I saw George put his head down while the commotion continued. I did the same. Finally, the men left and the service continued. After the service, Rumen led us to a van taking all of us to Sofia. Bouncing in white lawn chairs in the open back of the van, the driver careened around curves and straddled traffic lines making his way to Sofia. At least we were on the way out of the country.

New Beginnings Church in Shawnee, Oklahoma, led by Pastor Larry Sparks, agreed to put their arms around Grace Missionary Society to provide monthly support for the work. Little by little, others saw how we provided education, distributed food, and taught hygiene in Bulgaria so they supported the work financially.

I sensed the Spirit instructing Grace to open a preschool in which students could learn basic skills such as classroom behavior, hygiene, art, reading, and writing while enjoying one nutritious meal each day, all wrapped in a cape of Christian principles. No child was too old or too young to attend Grace Academy. We only required that one-fourth of the children who attended were from the ethnic Roma section of Nadezhda where the poorest, the naked Gypsies, resided. Aksenia, a retired public school teacher and believer accepted the position to teach. She used the Bible as her first textbook. We asked Rumen to oversee the program, and his wife, Zumbula, agreed to help with food preparation.

Aksenia's first task was to visit caregivers and persuade them that their children needed to go to school. After a few weeks, she amassed a classroom full of children. Aksenia took on the daily task of going to student's homes, sometimes waking them, helping them dress for school. About twenty children enrolled in the first semester. Later the school expanded to an afternoon class as well. After a few years, the school moved into a small basement room of a private home where the owner, Kapka, agreed to be the janitor and help serve the children food. Kapka did an excellent job despite suffering from bone cancer. After she faithfully served her family and Grace Academy for many years, she announced to a team visiting the school that doctors confirmed she was cancer free.

Aksenia also taught the children hygiene: how to wash their hands well, brush their teeth, comb their hair and take off their shoes, if they owned them, before entering the classroom. Seeing the accumulated grime on tiny hands, made me think about the old Lava soap Dad used to scrub off the motor oil on his hands and forearms. With too much scrubbing the pumice-laced soap could scrub the top layer of skin right off. I wished for some of this soap for the children, but the volcanic concoction was not available there. Instead, the children used antibacterial soap, brought to Bulgaria by team members who tucked it into their suitcases. Throughout the years many dentists sent small packs of toothbrushes and toothpaste. Combs were available in Bulgaria, but for two years we brought donated trial-sized bottles of shampoo and conditioner for families. One year, we bought shoes from the Shawnee, Oklahoma Kmart for fifty-cents a pair, packing them away in extra luggage space. The children and a few adults of Nadezhda enjoyed them. For the students who did not find a fit among the K-Mart shoes, shoes were bought.

Early in our service to the people of Nadezhda, George contacted the only doctor in Nadezhda, Dr. Kolev, to offer our assistance with medicine or equipment. After learning Dr. Kolev had few medications to dispense and received a salary of only seventy dollars a month for his work in the community, Grace Missionary Society took offerings to him every trip. Grace also gathered over-the-counter medications, bandages and other items to assist Dr. Kolev's ministry to the people of Nadezhda. We also sent funds through Danail to help Dr. Kolev purchase medication.

During his first trip to Bulgaria, Donnie noticed Dr. Kolev worked without a filing system for his growing clinic in Nadezhda so Grace sent funds to help him get organized. By that time, the clinic moved from its one-room, twelve-by-twelve building to a larger space in the administrative building of Nadezhda. Dr. Kolev also received a few raises in salary as the economy in Eastern Europe grew after joining the European Union. After twenty-years of Grace Missionary Society serving in Bulgaria, a pediatrician shares his practice with a new clinic in the planning stages of construction. During one visit, I asked Dr. Kolev if he was a Christian. "Of course," he answered as if I should have known. Dr. Kolev would eventually have two additional doctors to share the burden of care and received a significant raise in salary.

After the first five years of Grace Academy serving young children in Nadezhda, the Sliven Public School Minister of Education took note that the children from Nadezhda enrolling in public school came prepared to learn. After a few more years in Nadezhda, the first Roma graduated high school in Sliven, a student who started at Grace Academy. The first Roma honor roll student in Sliven Public Schools was a graduate of Grace Academy. A teacher from the public school system met with our team during one trip with one request: more schools.

We turned our attention to filling churches with children, which proved not quite as simple as hiring a good teacher and finding a place to hold classes, as we had done in Nadezhda. Under Communism, children were not allowed to go to church. When I asked village pastors about children's ministry, it was as if I spoke of a strange concept. Only the large churches were familiar with Sunday school or children's ministry. Five years into our work in Bulgaria and only a few children knew scripture. Something must be done.

When our sons were young, I taught Sunday school and children's church, but I certainly did not feel qualified to teach others how to best teach children. I prayed for wisdom because the Apostle James wrote, "If any of you lack wisdom, let him ask of God, that giveth to all men liberally, and upbraideth not; and it shall be given him" (James 1:5).

During a later trip to Bulgaria, I received a vision of teaching the concept of repentance. In my dream, I asked the children if they understood what repentance meant. They answered in the negative. I explained repentance means to turn around and go in a different direction. I shared an interactive story. Every time I mentioned the word repent, they turned around. Finally, I said, "Quit going away from God; turn around and follow Him."

Shortly after the dream, a lady in our home church presented a skit in which a dog barked and someone translated a lesson. This planted an idea. I ordered an adult-size St. Bernard dog suit. I wrote a skit based on my repent dream in which the dog character's bark was translated into words.

Then I wrote several more skits to teach various concepts of faith and unity.

My Bulgarian teams performed skits in churches and public parks using the dog suit. By the time Donnie traveled regularly with me to Bulgaria, his pseudo-identity became Sharro, a traditional Bulgarian name for a dog. Over the next few years, small teams engaged students in public schools, parks, and village churches. Along with Christian messages, the children quickly learned how to hit a piñata, a fun event introduced to them during the children's programs. Some teams also taught young believers to teach children Bible stories and concepts using puppetry.

Even before Grace Missionary Society outreach expanded into Bulgaria, the directors named Danail as administrator of funding. His advice and faithful communication with village pastors was necessary for accountability of funds and to provide oversight for the ministry. Danail was the necessary link to all Grace Missionary Society accomplishments in Bulgaria. When he married Dora, a certified accountant, she joined him in assisting with distribution of funds and record-keeping for Grace.

During one trip to Bulgaria, Danail drove our small group to the beautiful mountainous town of Kotel, where a church in the ski village needed much repair. Pastor Ivan served the church along with his pregnant wife, Luda, and their two sons. The young Ukrainian family struggled financially to take care of their family, the people in the congregation, and maintain facilities. Grace assisted with materials to spruce up the little church.

Pastor Sert later transferred to Nova Zagora, another city in Bulgaria. Grace continued assisting Ivan and Luda as they reached out to villages in that region. Tony, the man who first met George and Nathan when they arrived in Bulgaria to spy the land, and his wife Maria, eventually assumed the pastoral role in Kotel. With financial assistance through Grace Missionary Society, Tony and Maria, began an after-school program three afternoons each week. Two women in the church taught the children and teens. Their teaching positions provided a small income for their families.

Grace also financially assisted a Bulgarian man who went to villages to teach children scripture. Supporters helped him reach a generation before he suffered a stroke and could no longer travel. Some women also went to the villages to teach children reading and scriptures. Grace Missionary Society provided assistance with transportation expenses for them to drive to the villages.

Courage is not only for the young. Every season requires courage to move forward. Every generation must teach the next if God's Kingdom is to reseed itself. Mama's younger sister, Clarice, at seventy-one years old sensed the Spirit leading her to Bulgaria. This trip was her first outside the United States and Canada. While in the village of Mokren, Clarice noticed a woman carrying her child past the windows trying to listen to the music and sermon. Clarice's heart was moved because children had no place inside the church.

She went back to the United States and raised funds for materials to add a children's room onto the Mokren Church. The pastor at Mokren became so excited, he not only added a children's room, but also a youth room, pastor's office, and indoor toilets. After two years, the new facility was beautifully completed by the work of the men of the church with funds flowing through Grace Missionary Society for materials. The indoor toilets are still affectionately known as "Glenda's toilets" because I insisted they include them in the building project.

Clarice set the bar high for restoring small village church buildings in Bulgaria. After Mokren, we assisted many churches with repairs, restorations, and construction of church buildings. We learned a village was considered a Christian village if it had a Christian church building. It somehow established a presence of faith among the people of that village to have a permanent meeting space for communal worship.

Ministry to Bulgaria through Grace Missionary Society grew in unintentional ways. Sharon Baptist Church in Shawnee, Oklahoma, invited George, a young Bulgarian man attending Oklahoma Baptist University in Shawnee to speak one Sunday evening. My cousin Renda invited me to go with her. George sat on the front pew awaiting service to begin. I introduced myself to him and quickly gained a small amount of information about him.

George was completing his education in the United States with plans to return to Kazanlak, Bulgaria to assume leadership of a church his father pastored. New Beginnings Church invited George to assist with youth training. Buckled into the Bible belt, George later completed seminary at Baylor University in Waco, Texas, before returning home.

During his time in the United States, George became a friend to our family here in Oklahoma.

Over the years, Grace Missionary Society enjoyed many great times of fellowship and shared many meals with George, his parents, and later his beautiful wife, Laura. Under George's leadership and through designated offerings for his ministry, the church in Kazanlak added Sunday school rooms and a free medical clinic. The church began outreaches to the city through a winter food distribution for the elderly, hosted marriage seminars, offered numerous ministry teams, and assisted an orphanage for the deaf. Funds from several designated sources funded the ministry in Kazanlak.

George assigned members of his church to host visitors of the Grace team during Donnie's first trip to Bulgaria. Donnie and I stayed with a woman named Lehmah. Despite an obvious language barrier, Lehmah extended a big welcome to weary travelers on their first night in Kazanlak. With hand gestures, she welcomed me to take a bath. Ahhh. Of course. I gathered my towels and night clothes for what I expected to be a leisurely bath. Donnie planned to take the second shift.

As I undressed, Lehmah came into the bathroom. She helped me undress. She pulled a large round tub from the tiled shower and set a chair in it, motioning me to sit my naked self there. I obeyed. After filling buckets with warm water, she bathed my body, wiping it down with sponges filled with soap. Lehmah then plucked a brush from a shelf and scrubbed my skin. From head to toe, she scrubbed the top layer from my skin and rinsed me with clear water. My body turned red because of the scrubbing. She dried me with her own towels, and pulled out her own night clothes for me to wear. I knew the word "nay" so I insisted on wearing my own clothes. She slathered me with lotion, dusted me with powder and allowed me to pull my nightgown over my head before she dismissed me as having the full order of a Turkish bath.

Donnie decided he would not take a bath that night.

The next morning, Lehmah made lots of bread, bundled it up, and insisted we take it with us. As we waited in the lobby of her apartment while she gathered the bread, we discussed a loud ticking clock we heard overnight. When Lehmah returned to the foyer with bread bagged for our journey, I motioned to the clock. She got out a chair, pulled the U.S.S.R. made clock from the wall and insisted we take it with us. She did not allow "nay" this time. I later learned not to compliment people on things in their homes because they insisted on giving them to you as part of their generous hospitality.

On one visit to Bulgaria, my brother George noticed a young man going into the Bulgarian military asking for prayer in the Sliven Church. George felt the Lord tell him to go pray for the man named Alexander. George maintained contact with him during his military service. After the military, he returned to Sliven. With few jobs available, Alexander moved to England where his sister and family lived. He attended a Bulgarian church there and found a job so he could support himself and send money home to his mother.

Several years later, Grace Missionary Society received a note from Alexander asking for a little support to attend Youth With a Mission, a discipleship and training program for young ministers. After completing his training with YWAM, he returned to Bulgaria to serve the elderly and youth while caring for his mother.

Alexander introduced us to his uncle, Ilia, who pastored the church in the village of Koniovo. My heart rejoiced as through subsequent years of visiting this church, I watched the church develop and expand, even after Ilia and his wife suffered from failing health. Yet the health of the church is vibrant as it continues to meet for worship and reach out to other villages under the leadership of a local pastor.

A team from Life Church in Chickasha, Oklahoma, along with my son Gregory, granddaughters, Lillian and Delilah Grace, and cousin Darla Smith, formed a team to minister in the Stara Zagora Region of Bulgaria. It was the largest team ever taken to Bulgaria by Grace Missionary Society. The construction arm of the team was transported daily to a Nova Zagora Roma neighborhood church where they assisted with a church building project. The Chickasha team had also brought musicians who traveled to small churches in the Stara Zagora region where they encouraged several small village churches with their music and kind words.

The Chickasha team left after a week, but Gregory and his daughters, Darla and myself stayed in Bulgaria for a second week. Gregory drove an old yellow van to visit villages and pastors. This was the first time to be introduced to the village of Gavriolovo where Grace Missionary Society later partnered with the Sliven Church to construct a new church building. The congregation had been meeting in a metal storage container.

During each trip, every team added their prayers and personal touch to strengthen the churches of Bulgaria. Often it was just a group of three or four, on an administrative visit. Yet, with each visit relationships with the people evolved and the circle of acquaintances grew. I took them into my heart so deeply, each one became an extension of family.

Through more than twenty years of serving the church and people of Bulgaria through Grace Missionary Society, many family members and friends came alongside to help. Some gave financially to the work. Others actually traveled there to add their personal gifting to the cause. Kathy Palmer-Harris traveled with teams three times. She never wavered in her financial and prayerful support of Grace Missionary Society outreaches. Bruce and his wife, Verna, also never wavered in their financial and prayerful support. James Palmer also traveled to Bulgaria, later allowing his youngest son, Austin to join a team. James and his wife, Brenda, faithfully financially supported the Grace Missionary Society. My cousin Darla Stone Smith accepted the title of president of Grace Missionary Society after George and

Shirley retired from their positions. For a while, cousin Renda Kever took the treasurer post and joined one team. It was a family knit together with purpose in which others came alongside to add their gifts. As mission director, I was given freedom to serve as the Spirit of God prompted me, but not without knowing so many individuals and churches were covering me constantly in prayer. They were tolerant of my weaknesses and rejoiced at successes for the people of Bulgaria.

Darla traveled to Bulgaria three times, one trip included the niece of Sister Honeywell who taught me why I needed Jesus and inspired me to learn to play the accordion. I contacted Joyce Priest a few years earlier to thank her for coming to McLoud with her Aunt Sarah when I was just a child to teach me the power of God's Word. After telling her what we were doing, she joined a team of three women who held a women's conference in Kotel, Bulgaria. That conference was live streamed to Italy.

There are too many donors and people who committed to pray for our service to mention. Suffice it to say family, friend, and stranger support was unconditional and faithful.

Danail, who first came alongside Grace to teach young Roma men English, has never wavered in his support and administrative service for this organization. Those of us who knew him in the beginning watched as he matured, served in the military, married his beautiful wife, Dora, and they had their children. Danail and Dora have visited our homes in Oklahoma and we often stay in their home when we go to Bulgaria. Daniel's accountability is impeccable. As with so many of the pastors who came alongside Grace in the beginning, he remained faithful to the Kingdom task of building up the churches of Bulgaria, strengthening them, and laboring with them.

During my first trip to Bulgaria, the Spirit had spoken to my heart that the task of Grace Missionary Society was to build up the churches of Bulgaria for the time when we could no longer go there. Doors continued to open. Grace Missionary Society became a multi-tasking organization with small projects which strengthened the evangelical churches of Bulgaria. For the past twenty years, Grace Missionary Society assisted with construction or remodeling of numerous village churches, while continuing the education of children and adults, feeding the hungry, training children's ministers, discipling believers, providing pastoral training, assisting with employment readiness. In short, when we saw a need, we filled it.

The Roma people ministered to through Grace, who traveled to other countries to find employment or education met as a church group and continued to drop seeds of the love of God wherever they traveled, establishing small congregations of family and friends that grew to reach out to those in the cities where they found work, including many cities and villages in Europe.

Our work in Bulgaria meant moving large stone walls of prejudices and traditions so the church could work together to serve people of all ages in all stages of life. By joining the European Union, Bulgaria flourished economically. However, change comes slow for the poor. There is still much to do.

*****

It was as if all my life I had been waiting and preparing for this moment when I could spend my latter years on the earth for this purpose. My intention was, and will remain, to serve the people of Bulgaria until the Lord gathers me to Himself. Meanwhile, even as the work in Bulgaria flourished, others needed to be reached too.

In prayer one day, the Spirit showed me the Psalms 2:8 (Amplified Bible), "Ask of me and I will give you the nations."

I answered, "I am asking, Lord."

He always answers. My anchor was in McLoud, but my sight had been lifted to include the nations.

Chapter 24
Meanwhile Back Home

"I will pour out my Spirit on your offspring, and my blessing on your descendants. They will spring up like grass in a meadow, like poplar trees by flowing streams."
Isaiah 44: 3-4, NIV

Both our sons married in 1998, six months apart. I first traveled to Bulgaria in November 2000. Gregory and Lana expected their first child in December. I was only home from Bulgaria about two weeks when Lillian Lucille arrived on December 1, 2000. Delilah Grace was born to Gregory and Lana on June 8, 2002.

With our sons married and ministry in Bulgaria going well, I looked again into earning the college degree my heart ached to hold. Over the years I took classes off and on at Rose State College in Midwest City, the college constructed in the seventies that I'd hoped to attend. An incomplete goal is always hanging out there urging its creator to finalize.

St. Gregory's University was located only eleven miles from McLoud. I met with a counselor who asked me to bring him a complete list of my experiences and education. With two filled three-ring binders of resumes and supporting documents, I headed to his office. When I plopped my bundle on his desk, he quickly told me to condense. Since I scanned in photos, brought VHS tapes of television appearances, and copies of newsletters I wrote, along with certificates of classes, he accepted my application for the program without reading my tons of material. All he really wanted to see were my college transcripts. With no intentions to do so, I had logged my adult life in this binder and my words during nine years of combined newspaper work.

By spring 2003, donned in cap and gown, I walked the stage to receive a Bachelor of Social Science degree finishing magna cum laude, and was named by my professors as Student of the Year for the adult education program.

Granddaughters Lillian and Delilah attended the graduation with their parents, Gregory and Lana. It was an amazing day, a culmination of many years of hope becoming a reality. Mama did not come to the ceremony, but she congratulated me on finally finishing.

Donnie retired from Tinker Air Force Base Fire Department in 2001, but I wasn't ready to retire. Heartland Home Health allowed me to combine my licensed practical nursing technical degree with my social science degree for a position as a medical social worker, working with a licensed social supervisor to provide oversight. I loved the job. It seemed as if I did at home what Grace Missionary Society did in its outreaches: help people find resources to assist with living better quality lives.

Donnie and I packed away unnecessary and outdated items we accumulated during our lives in McLoud. With two granddaughters, and another on the way, and the special gift of a goddaughter from Rick and Amy Sanders, I made room for sleepovers and tea parties. Plastic containers became history-savers as I filled each with trophies, baseball cards, soccer pads, and airplane models, each symbolizing one son's individual childhood interests and involvements. In the process of storing tokens of their youth, I found boxes of photos, research papers, mementos of my years on the newspaper, and personal treasures. I was about to set them aside for future consideration, when I heard the voice. I knew in my heart that when I died, our sons would throw these McLoud tokens into the trash without any thought of them being historically valuable.

McLoud offered no organization to collect its history. Leah Horton Bird wrote a book on the communities of McLoud and Dale called, *Two Communities in Stitches* published in 1971, but McLoud offered no centralized place for collections or to market the city's history through her book.

Donnie served on the McLoud City Council for eight years during which the Council tried to fulfill each suggestion of a comprehensive plan compiled in 1989. Somehow, the suggested historical preservation organization always ended up on the shelf, begging for someone to initiate it.

I envisioned an old house to display the rich history of our town. Donnie and I owned several rent houses at the time, which funded our traveling through Grace Missionary Society and personal travel, so it seemed plausible. I held no qualification for historical preservation, no training, no preconceived idea of how it should be done. All I knew to do was step into the water and see what God would do and who He would use to make it a reality. I figured if He assigned me this task, He would surely show me the steps to take to reach the other side. I called a few friends and asked them to join me in a meeting. I asked four people to serve on a board of directors. With some coaxing, each agreed to serve on the board to begin a new preservation journey for their community. With the initial boost of a few helpers, I believed McLoud could support a historical society.

I made a trip to Prague, Oklahoma to visit Mama's brother. Uncle Cleo played an instrumental role in initiating a historical society there. He furnished me with proposed by-laws, sharing bits of do's and don't's he'd learned. After contacting the Internal Revenue Service for instructions to set up a non-profit, we formed the society. The support of many people who shared love and respect for the community and those who chose to invest their lives in McLoud cemented the building blocks for the new endeavor. The voice reminded me His first instruction to my heart was to bury myself in the community of McLoud. I reminded the voice I had already served through the newspaper, by being Chamber of Commerce secretary for nine years, and owning a small business when Donnie and I built McLoud Self-Storage. Was He asking me to do more?

It never occurred to me not to try. Mama always told us, "Can't never could do nothin' without they tried." But it needed many hands and hearts to gather and save one hundred years of history. I like to refer to those who participated in the McLoud Historical Society using the pronoun "we." We were in it together. We appreciated each contributor. We were a team. However, I will mention by name those who made monumental impacts on the development of McLoud Historical Society.

My sister, Kathy Palmer-Harris was the first to accept the position as secretary and began taking notes at all meetings. After a short time of being treasurer, retired teacher Iris Dial, handed the books to Jim Metcalf. Jim's wife, Sylvia, whose family lived several generations in McLoud, became the curator and art director. Jim Walker and Jon Barrett, both McLoud High School graduates whose families were rooted deeply in McLoud accepted Board of Director positions, which they have held to the time of this writing.

With the announcement that an organization was forming to save history, it suddenly became known among the coffee drinkers as "the hysterical society." Our little hysterical group met monthly to discuss options and the fundraisers began.

A former Ford dealership on the corner of 5th Street and Broadway in McLoud was an eye-sore on the main highway through McLoud for many years. Boarded windows and crumbling frontage made the town center appear unkept. I found the building owner's contact information at the County Assessor's office. I phoned the owner who agreed he would be willing to sell for a historical project. After a little negotiation from a friend of the museum, the owner agreed to sell to the Society for eighty-thousand dollars.

Oklahoma celebrated its centennial that year, 2007. McLoud High School Alumni Judy Sell, who had accepted a vacated position on the Board of Directors, learned of a grant for historical preservation from funds set aside specifically for the state's centennial celebration, so she initiated the application process. Later in the year, a representative of the Centennial Commission granted fifty-thousand dollars to the McLoud Historical Society. With what we earned through fundraisers, memberships and donations, and with many people contributing, the Society matched the grant with thirty-thousand dollars to purchase the building at 421 W. Broadway in McLoud. Without Judy's perseverance and God's timing on this grant the building would not have been purchased.

The Society closed on the building in November 2007 with grant terms that the museum must be open by April 2008. The first large donation came in February: ten-thousand dollars in concrete and labor to raise the floor in the front bay. Judy and her friend Don Morris worked out a remodeling plan for the building, including an office area, front bay, back bay, landscaping and signage. Together, they promoted historical preservation using their technology skills. Many people spent hundreds of hours working on the front bay, scraping walls, tearing out debris, repairing leaks. It was an enormous task made less overwhelming by the many hands and hearts who labored, compensated only by the satisfaction of doing good for their fellow McLoud citizens. Donnie Kuhn and Jim Metcalf, along with many others carried the load of much of the physical labor.

McLoud had much to uncover and celebrate. It holds the title of Blackberry Capital of the World. The first female pharmacist in Oklahoma co-owned a pharmacy in McLoud, and the first female bank president in Oklahoma headed the McLoud Bank of Commerce. One of the oldest women in the United States, 117-year-old Belle Bivins, lived in McLoud. Famous baseball players and football players called McLoud their hometown.

Judy Sell contacted the Potawatomi Tribe, who assisted the Society in ongoing ways including windows. Judy also contacted former McLoud residents who donated and installed overhead doors. These two donations maintained the historical integrity of the building. Many citizens participated in fundraisers, Sunday dinners, quilt shows, plant sales, and garage sales. McLoud Masonic Lodge matched funds raised with their sponsorship. Recognition plaques were etched for individuals and businesses giving large donations. All these funding streams provided for other needs during the remodeling. Little by little, the McLoud Historical Society Museum and Heritage Center bloomed. Little by little, the big old building continued its seemingly miraculous transformation into one of the most beautiful buildings in town.

By July 2010, the Society transformed the front bay of the old garage into an area for permanent displays. Ava Keene, a McLoud High School Alumnus donated antique display cases for showcasing pieces of McLoud history. Donnie and I and Jim and Sylvia made the trek to Weatherford, Oklahoma, to load and pick up the cases. City employees and McLoud Telephone Company employees helped unload. Then, Jim and Sylvia Metcalf, and Donnie Kuhn went to work to restore the cases. Meanwhile Sylvia used her artistic skills to create pleasing-to-the eye displays. Jim used his carpenter skills for nearly every project, including the later addition of a kitchen, restroom and old barn display. He and Sylvia were faithful with their support and applied skills. Donnie Kuhn would spend his retirement years painting, cleaning, planning, and doing hard labor on the building. For several years, Donnie gathered and cleaned metal and donated funds to the museum project.

I must emphasize here, I only played a part with any of the wonderful things that happened for the McLoud Historical Society. The organization wobbled often, but remained in motion. It seemed an idea or need would be suggested and someone or a business stepped up to do it. State Representatives and Senators promoted the historical project both in donations and connections. Copper penny awnings were the result of one of these connections. The McLoud Chamber of Commerce, BancFirst of McLoud, McLoud Telephone Company, McLoud City Hall, churches and individuals stepped up to help, each adding their own gifts and skill sets to make this project a reality.

McLoud Historical Society helped the City of McLoud apply for a grant for sidewalk upgrades in the heart of town. With assistance from the McLoud city clerk and board of trustees, the sidewalk project became a reality. Downtown McLoud looked much better.

Historical preservation is a gift to the community. If humans cannot look back, how can they envision their future? Only history and hope can connect this mystery.

From my childhood, I learned that knowing you are loved is not the same as knowing you are valued. Love can often be emotional. Value is purposeful. People can only begin to comprehend love when they sense they are valued by their Creator and their fellow man. I wanted the people of McLoud to know they are valued.

They are worth a beautiful downtown.

They are worthy of growth and development.

The individuals and businesses committed to building McLoud, Oklahoma, are worth the investment of the time and talents of those who committed to this project.

The second phase of remodeling the old Ford dealership began. Donnie Kuhn, Sylvia Metcalf, Jim Metcalf, and Kathy Harris continued to serve through the McLoud Historical Society to the date of this writing. Aaron Capps and Dean Hill later joined the Board. Other board members who served for short periods of time, included Norma Higdon, Phyllis Campbell, and Karen Baade. Businesses too numerous to mention, local organizations, and generous individuals served tirelessly, faithfully honoring the past, present and future of our community.

*****

Mama's health was failing. Grace Missionary Society and McLoud Historical Society responsibilities pressed upon me. I retired from my position in home health so I could give more attention to Mama's needs and focus on the non-profits.

As memorabilia and history grew, our family grew too. Three more granddaughters were added, Emmaline Jeanette, Cecilia Rose and Aliyah Selah.

Our private lives at home became filled with laughter as Donnie and I enjoyed sleepovers, kids' movies, tea parties, and trips with the grands. I wrote and published a children's book about each granddaughter's interest. *Friend Philia* is based on Lillian's relationship with her dog, Philia. *Delilah Dances - One Step at a Time* tells the story of a young girl who learned perseverance is the way to develop a new skill. I based *Powerful Emajen-ation* on the concept of respect for others that Emmaline learned as a kindergartener. *Sir Locksalot Loses His Keys* featured characters who share names with Cecilia Rose and focuses on responsibility. *Aliyah Likes Being a Giraffe* is a lesson in self-acceptance. There are still some children's stories in my queue not yet completed. Maybe in the winter season of my life.

All rivers of life flowed simultaneously -- to my family, the community, and the world -- creating one very active triune force. Juggling the joy of growing Grace Missionary Society, McLoud Historical Society and grandchildren seemed like a rushing mountain stream fed by clear waters emerging into one flow, bouncing over rocks and tumbling through rivulets to journey together. I found a deep pool along the fountain flowing within me; my joy was full, spirit, soul and body.

During the twenty years of Grace Missionary Society expanding around the world, with their parent's blessing, Donnie and I took each of our granddaughters to a place of their choice when they turned ten years old. Lillian chose Alaska. Delilah Grace chose Washington, D.C. Emmaline chose to go to Paris, France, and her parents decided to tag along. Cecilia took off with us to New Mexico for a balloon festival and train ride through the Rockies. Aliyah took us to Padre Island in South Texas.

Glenda Palmer-Kuhn

Donnie and I also traveled to many other states and countries enjoying seeing new places and meeting new people. Praying for each country we traveled through was a natural pleasure for me.

Chapter 25
India

"Then I heard the voice of the Lord saying, 'Whom shall I send? And who will go for us?' And I said, 'Here am I. Send me!'" Isaiah 6:8 NIV

As my vision indicated, I touched India in 2013. Like a hot iron, just a brush scarred my soul. As George, Shirley, Vani Palmer, and I disembarked the plane in Chennai, India, the smell hit me first, the scent of curry mingled with sweat, unknown spices, automobile exhaust, and salty sea air. My brain made no sense of the mingle of odors my nose inhaled.

My personal journey to Asia began eight years earlier when a man living in west Texas asked George for assistance with financial support for small churches in India. Prasanna owned a medical laboratory in Odessa, Texas. He financially assisted his family in India while living the American dream with his wife and children in the United

States. His first wife died in an automobile accident, leaving him a single parent of a daughter. Prasanna established a church in India to honor his wife. He traveled to India often to visit family and oversee the church. While searching for support for the family and churches of India, Prasanna found Grace Missionary Society on the internet and followed up by contacting George.

Grace always traveled to a place before Grace Missionary Society pledged any financial support because we wanted to personally meet and build a relationship with church leaders to ascertain whether it was a good place to plant donor funds. Again, George went on a spying adventure to India to check out the land. He met with several pastors who had no outside financial support. Many of them gathered in huts or open-air venues in small villages and hamlets of South India, specifically Andhra Pradesh, one of the poorest in India and one which persecuted many Christians.

The board of directors for Grace Missionary Society decided to assist trained evangelists by sending them out with a bicycle and a megaphone to plant a church. Some villages had churches but simply needed a sponsor.

Most believers in India were widows or the desperately poor searching for hope among the numerous gods of their country. Like the apostle Paul, we wanted to introduce them to the God and Father of the Lord Jesus Christ and establish a centralized, pastor-led church attached to a larger church for oversight and discipleship. It was the goal of Grace Missionary Society to teach the people how to live out their faith every day.

One of Prasanna's family groups opened a school named Good Shepherd. Grace sought and found sponsors, allowing the school to purchase food, plates, and eating utensils to replace banana leaves for serving the food. Most of the children were not orphans, but from very poor households.

At the time, Grace didn't have the budget to expand into Indian church planting, so Grace Missionary Society invited sponsors to support each pastor in training. Once a church gathered and had a sponsor, we sent a monthly salary to the founding pastor along with widow and orphan support. Grace set goals for the local churches: meet in a permanent place, offer a means of transportation for the pastor, and make the churches self-supporting within three years.

George, Shirley, Donnie, and I learned three years was not a realistic goal for equipping pastors to sustain churches. However, faithfulness to these young congregations helped most of them eventually reach those goals. One pastor, Melchizedek, father of four sons, had a small sponsorship to supplement what Grace provided for his congregation and family. Melchizedek's brother, Levi, had four daughters. His small church gathered in his home to worship. His only sponsorship was Grace. Two women who gathered believers together in their respective villages received sponsors. Grace found sponsors for two more pastors whose congregations also met in huts. In total, ten churches and one school, Good Shepherd, were sponsored by Grace. Each church grew in numbers, but the one flourishing the most was pastored by Jeevan Babu, and named for their sponsor, George Palmer House of Prayer.

It seemed a natural division for Grace Missionary Society at that time, that George coordinated most of the outreach financial sponsorship for India, while I focused on Bulgaria. Along with Shirley and counsel from United States pastors and friends, Grace purchased motorcycles for transportation. Churches flourished on Indian time, slow and steady.

George and Shirley made several trips to India before I traveled there. Some sponsoring American church pastors also traveled to India with them.

Eventually, George and Shirley's son, Nathan, married Vani, a woman from India, daughter of the Good Shepherd school overseers, and niece to Prasanna. She moved to Oklahoma with Nathan and obtained citizenship in the United States.

Vani used our 2013 trip to India to visit her family. George and Shirley Palmer, Vani Palmer and I made the long flight. Her family met us at our first stop in Chennai to pick up their daughter and sister and return to the Mangalagieri area until we arrived later in the trip. We stayed in a lovely hotel in Chennai.

After Vani left with her happy family, we traveled south to the state of Andhra Pradesh where George reserved rooms at the Hotel Central Park in the city of Ongole.

I watched humanity from the second-story window of a two-star hotel in Ongole. From my perch, I observed a street and a city park. In the park, among the overgrown vegetation, I saw a shack of sorts, made of cardboard and scrap wood. In front of the shack a young Indian teen washed himself by dipping a cloth in water and wiping his flesh. Another young man emerged and took his turn at the water bucket, sloshing it over his body from a cup he dipped into the receptacle.

Below on the street, hundreds of people passed by on their way somewhere. Slumped-over elderly women picked up plastic waste putting it in a carrier on their backs. Men in suits walked quickly. Some stopped to urinate on the grass beside the sidewalk before continuing along the concrete path. Young women walked past carrying books or large bags. No one looked at each other or seemed to notice the men who stopped to relieve themselves. The only children I saw from the window were the boys outside the shack bathing themselves. They buttoned up their shirts and joined the crowd of walkers.

The spiritual climate was heavy, very heavy. I felt smothered by the sense that the humans I watched did not live, but simply existed. It seemed I looked into the throat of hell where people had not yet descended but seemed destined to go. They danced around the lips of it, hoping someone would notice them. I wept.

George, Shirley, and I went to breakfast before hiring a driver to take us to D.G.Peta, a village in the mountains above Ongole, near the tiger refuge, where the snake-catchers hunted their livelihood. The long arduous trip led us into the darkness of India, but, we heard of light among the darkness. A pastor led a small hut church in a small village named C.S.Puram.

The pastor's son, Jonathan, a boy of about sixteen, greeted us with graciousness. A member of a snake catcher family attended an outdoor worship service the pastor organized. Pastor Prakasam said she and her children could lose their lives for being at the Christian service, yet they came. We greeted the church, then prayed for those who wanted prayer, including the young snake catcher and her children.

We descended the mountain just like we ascended: in a small vehicle over rough, one-lane roads through small communities where people huddled in groups as if waiting for something or someone.

George and Shirley shared a room at the hotel in Ongole. I stayed alone. I had been warned by human trafficking reports that women traveling alone are sometimes lured from their rooms and taken captive for ransom or to sell. That night at the hotel in Ongole, I received a phone call in my room. In heavily accented English, the caller told me I had a note at the front desk. Thinking this was out of the ordinary, I ignored it. After about fifteen minutes, I received a second call.

Perhaps, I thought, *there is an emergency at home.*

I phoned George's room and asked for his advice. He offered none.

But, I remembered the scripture, "He will have no fear of bad news; his heart is steadfast, trusting in the LORD" (Psalm 112: 7 NIV). So, I ignored it again.

Then someone put a note under my door.

I believed someone was trying to lure me out of my room. The calls didn't stop. After another hour of phone calls and another note, I dressed and made my way to the front desk. Evidently, those who attempted to lure me out gave up and left. They left a note similar to the one under my door: a name with a phone number. I returned to my hot room. I slept fitfully, waking often from nightmares of dark rooms with no way of escape. By morning, I felt haggard and very tired.

When I met George and Shirley in the dining room for breakfast, I could hardly look at the steaming pots of gray or red liquids with vegetables and fish floating inside. It reminded me of the fish gravy Mama made for Dad. The smell made my appetite flee like a swatted gnat. George asked for eggs and bread for breakfast, so I survived on that. We drank only sealed bottled water and hot drinks. Being a fan of chai, I ordered a cup, which tasted heavenly because it was steeped in very warm water and buffalo milk. Like Pastor Prakasam in D.G.Peta, with food as with people, one can usually discover a bright spot.

George, Shirley and I took a small taxi-type vehicle to the train station for the next leg of our journey to the city of Guntur. We could not read the signs and did not know which train to take. Basically, we were lost at the train station, filled with shoulder-to-shoulder people while trains waited on multiple tracks.

George noticed a man passing out flyers and asked for directions. Miraculously, the man spoke English. He was also a pastor using flyers to invite people to church. *Thank you, Lord!* In broken but understandable English, he told us which train to take and the time it departed.

We arrived in Guntur to familiar faces and lots of Indian chatter. Pastor Levi's family met us and directed us to our hotel. Their excitement encouraged us, and we appreciated their gifts of fruit. Other, less friendly people waited for us at the hotel; George pointed out the government agents in suits who'd watched us since Ongole.

The next day George, Shirley, and I traveled to the village of Pastor Levi where his wife served us the best food of our trip, tiger rice. Pastor Levi and his wife introduced us to their children and some people who attended their small home church. This was the first place a family gave me the honor of naming a child. The little girl became Abigail Lilly, her name meaning beautiful, intelligent flower.

Following the visit in Guntur, we proceeded to a hotel in Vijayawada, watching the men in suits peer from the second floor balcony. I waited to meet Elvis Wynters, the young boy, now a man, who Donnie and I sponsored years before through Mission of Mercy. He took a train from Calcutta to meet me in person for the first time.

As I waited for Elvis, my mind rehearsed the events leading me to this place and time. How on earth did my travel to meet a man I sponsored as a child lead to my being watched by government agents? In our first three days in India, I traveled up a mountain for a worship service where snake catchers lived in danger, someone attempted to lure me from my hotel room, and I saw humanity in its base existence. I stared down grotesque temples and encountered a brother in Christ in a most unlikely train station. Now, here I was in a beautiful hotel in Vijayawada where I could be charged with espionage.

Elvis stepped through the front door of the hotel, and we greeted one another. It felt a bit awkward at first, then absolutely comfortable as if I had known him since he was a child. George and Shirley retired to their room while Elvis and I walked down the unfamiliar streets of Vijaywada on our way to dinner at Kentucky Fried Chicken if we survived out-of-control traffic along the way.

From Vijayawada, George, Shirley, Elvis and I traveled by open-air taxis to villages served by Grace-sponsored pastors. We enjoyed more time with the brothers, Melchizedek and Levi, and their families, sharing a meal with each one. George booked rooms at a gated resort near where Vani's family lived. Once we arrived at the apartments, I felt safe for the first time on the trip.

Vani's family was friendly. They showed us where the Good Shepherd kids once gathered when Grace sponsored the school. They hoped to reorganize it and serve children again. We shared meals with them in the evenings, but during the day, we traveled to other villages served by Grace pastors.

We ate rice in many forms and drank coconut milk from the shell. We caught our first sighting of monkeys in their native habitat. The creatures played in a tree, one I could see just outside the window of the church where we ate tiger rice and village children entertained us by singing.

While visiting the George Palmer House of Prayer, pastored by Jeevan Babu, another family gave me the honor of naming a little girl. I named her Hope Joy because I hoped that the joy of the Lord would strengthen the churches of India.

A highlight of the trip to South India was visiting the place where St. Thomas established a Christian enclave before he was martyred. Pieces of his bones had been saved as relics on display.

Suddenly, as if we had just arrived, it was time to go home. We prepared to leave for the United States via Chennai. I sensed this was my only visit to India, and a final farewell to Elvis pulled at my emotions. Finally, I met the man, who was a boy of eighteen when I last sponsored him. Now, he taught English and art. He left to return to his home outside Calcutta.

Vani's brothers insisted on taking us to the train. Trains might be the only punctual thing in India, and we must make the train to Chennai where we reserved a hotel for the night because our flight left for the U.S. the following afternoon. What should have been a nice drive became a street race through narrow, winding, slightly-paved roads at a very fast pace because Vani's brothers picked us up late from the resort.

As we raced to the train, I prayed, *Lord, help us make this connection.* Between teeth grinding near escapes in traffic and jammed roadways, we finally made it in time for the last call to board. We raced up the stairs, urging Vani to say quick goodbyes and join us in the race for the United States. We made it. Just barely. Thanks be to God.

Early the next morning in Chennai, Shirley called me to come over to their room because she thought George was having a heart attack. Pulling on my clothes, I ran down the hall where George lay groaning with head pain, holding his ears, and complaining of dizziness. Hotel staff arrived with a wheelchair, transporting him by elevator to the ground floor where a taxi awaited. On the way to the hospital, between groans of pain and vertigo, George told me if anything happened to him to cremate him and bury him in India.

"I'm not going to do that," I said. "We have a plane to catch."

Shirley and I followed the ambulance in a taxi, arriving just in time to see the doctor. His heart rate was slow, but his pressure was good. Ultimately, the doctor diagnosed George with an inner ear infection and dehydration and gave him medication. The cost? Less than ten dollars, which included heart tests, an injection and four prescriptions.

Just as my vision revealed. I touched India, and now I was home again. We all survived.

Chapter 26
The Nations

"Ask of me and I will make the nations your inheritance." Psalm 2:8, NIV

Quilts for comfort to Turkey, Greece, and the Navajo

Geography was not one of my strongest subjects in high school. In adulthood, I excused my lack of knowledge of borders and beyond by saying it was because the geography teachers were usually coaches, more interested in the next game than the next country. I could find Greece on a map because Jackie Kennedy married a Greek after President John F. Kennedy's assassination. Greece was surrounded by beautiful Mediterranean waters pocked with enchanting islands. I even learned a few Greek words by researching their meaning in the New Testament.

Greece's next-door neighbor was Turkey. Beyond that, I knew the nations by name only from coloring world maps in fourth grade. I admit my ignorance, but the calling of God is not limited by my knowledge, nor is it limited by government-placed borders.

In the late 1980s, I heard about missionaries in the Greek city of Piraeus. I wrote them a letter, and they answered. I could not send much money, but I did begin a pen pal communication with them.

The First Assembly of God in McLoud offered separate youth group discipleship classes on Wednesday nights for girls and boys. I wanted to help with the girls, but I possessed limited knowledge of arts and crafts. So, I did the only thing I knew to do at the time: we tacked quilts. The girls sat around the quilt and tied the knots while we talked about the Word. They were free to ask anything as we discussed scripture within the framework of current events and their personal lives. We sent one of the quilts they tacked to the missionaries in Piraeus, Greece.

The girls received a wonderful letter of thanks for the gift. The missionaries, a young couple with two small children, wrote of the blessing to have some comfort from home in the United States. The family visited our home about five years later when they returned from Greece to itinerate.

Many hands worked, so many quilts were made. I did not know where to distribute them all. One day, a man visiting the McLoud area to gather items to take to the Navajo Nation heard we made quilts. He asked if I would like to send some to the Navajo. Thinking of the selflessness of Sister Honeywell, now deceased, I readily agreed that giving to the Navajo would be like returning comfort from the woman who brought it from the Navajo Nation to me in McLoud. So the young girls and I tacked a big stack of quilts and sent them to the Navajo just in time for Christmas. I personally contacted the missionaries who served there for verification of their needs before sending them by courier. From them, I learned they liked to give a quilt to each family for Christmas and it was the perfect timing to send them. The girls helped gather other items to send such as, socks, small toys, toothbrushes, and toothpaste.

Even though these events took place long before Grace Missionary Society formed, it seemed like these days were seeds planted in the hearts of senders and receivers alike, little ways of being a blessing and becoming one. These were my first steps of reaching out beyond the borders of my hometown.

I reflected fondly on the years of quilting with the young women of the McLoud First Assembly of God youth group when we first went to Bulgaria. One of the first things we did was introduce the Turkish women in Nadezhda to piecing quilts. Grace bought a sewing machine and hired a sewing teacher. A pastor in Nadezhda went to neighboring Turkey to purchase cotton fabric needed for the sewing class. Every quilt boasted tan squares because he bought a large full bolt of tan cotton for the ladies. He added smaller amounts of forest green and dull blue. These colors were mingled with scraps of fabric I carried in luggage from the United States.

Some of the ladies sewed for the first time and earned their first wage. Turkey was only about fifty miles from Sliven, Bulgaria. The vision of a man sitting on a hillside asking for someone to tell him about Jesus Christ kept pulling at my heart. As Americans, we were not allowed to cross the border into Turkey without a visa. God answered our prayers for Turkey by introducing the Grace board of directors to a non-denominational evangelist/pastor in Turkey named Engin. He published a book of his testimony of faith in Jesus Christ. He met with men in coffee shops where he shared his faith and passed out copies of his testimonial book. He eventually established a home church group and discipled new believers.

Members of Grace Missionary Society also prayed earnestly for Engin and his family. While suffering from a blood disease, he continued to evangelize in public places such as park benches and coffee houses. Engin, and his family, and a small group of believers held Christmas events at malls to introduce the public to Jesus Christ. His wife reached out to women in the neighborhoods where they lived. When the congregation grew, Engin turned the vibrant believers over to another pastor while he and his family went out to establish another work among Turkish and Kurdish people.

Engin was healed from his blood disease. His energy levels returned to allow him to remain active with personal evangelism and church planting. Grace continues to financially support them.

Africa

Fellow missionaries who attended New Beginnings Church in Shawnee, Oklahoma served in Malawi. They traveled there several times with teams, but sensed the Spirit instructing them to begin a new work serving orphans and widows. They called their organization Hope House Orphan Care, funding the work through child sponsorship.

Feeding orphans and widows in the poorest country on the African continent seemed overwhelming, but these two servants decided to step into the Jordan and see what miracle God would open up before them.

One Sunday, they made a presentation about their work in Malawi. I sensed the Lord speaking that neither Grace Missionary Society nor I should sponsor a child, but that I should ask directors Jim and Janelle what big thing they needed to get set up for feeding and educating children. They answered that they needed a building separate from the little church with some land for expansion and gardening. They knew of land with a building for sale for over three thousand dollars. Grace Missionary Society donated the cost of the building.

Both Jim and Janelle traveled to Bulgaria with teams. Their ministry in Malawi continues.

*****

United States

New Beginnings Church Pastor Larry Sparks along with his wife, Vicki, joined a team ministering to an inner city in

Delaware. Vicki put together Bible school training materials and crafts, while husband and wife team, James and Josie planned enough all-American hotdog and chip meals to feed a passel of hungry children. Pastors of New Hope Baptist Mission in Delaware coordinated the team project to host a Bible school in the heart of the crime-ridden district in Wilmington. My niece Billie Jo Palmer from Heavener, Oklahoma went along to help as did others from New Beginnings Church in Shawnee, including Ken and Elaine, and the Sparks' grandson, Cody.

Each day the group broke into sub-groups and made prayer walks through the neighborhood. People sitting on porches whispered their curiosity to each other as they watched us pass the first day. By the next walk-by, they became fully aware of why we visited the neighborhood. Some asked for team members to pray with them, especially for the sick. Some made professions of faith.

One day during a neighborhood Bible school in Wilmington, police burst through the front door of a row house where our team was hosting the bible school. Guns were drawn as they pushed past children seated around a kitchen table. Excusing themselves, they bolted through the back kitchen door into a small enclosed yard where they thought someone might be hiding. Once the police passed through, we continued with Bible school. The children acted as if such disruptions were common.

Following the last day of Bible school, the team joined Chad and Matilda in their country home to spend the night. Team members enjoyed a trip to Rehoboth Beach the next day. On the way to the airport, the team spent time in Philadelphia.

Billie Jo and I joined another team the next summer. We saw some of the same faces and met new Bible school attendees. We did not experience any police chases through the front door to the backyard during the second visit. There was, however, an armed robbery at a small convenience store across the street from the Bible school.

I contemplated these one-week projects, analyzing the value of the days spent and how much could be accomplished. I concluded that by going, each of us planted seeds. I trusted the Holy Spirit to bring light and life to those seeds so they could grow in the hearts of the children we touched.

*****

Brazil

For about a year during my first part-time employment at *The McLoud News*, I learned about a group looking for volunteers to send Bibles to Brazil. The group furnished the Bibles, packaging, and addresses. Volunteers filled the packages and added an address before paying the postage to mail it to South America. Like planting seeds, the anticipation of someone receiving a Bible, reading it, and finding Christ filled me with much joy. From the new little office Donnie made for me from enclosing part of the front porch, I sent one Bible a week for eighteen months. Even though I would never truly know if the seed sprouted, I prayed for good soil and a bountiful blessing from the Word of God. Like watering and plucking weeds, praying for Brazil became part of my heart's prayers.

After the sons were grown and on their own, Donnie and I joined a team from New Beginnings Church traveling up the Amazon River. When the team reached the airport in Oklahoma City, the airline told us we must wait two days because the plane was overbooked.

Disappointed and a bit angry, we went back home to wait, the delay diverted us away from the planned destination to minister to a remote tribe. I found it difficult to keep telling myself God's timing is not diminished by airline schedules, but is often confirmed by change and delay.

Our team met up with others in the modern city of Manaus. As we boarded the boat taking our team and others up a flooded river, the boat captain advised us to choose a hammock where each person would sleep during the trip. Following introductions, the boat's engine burped on. Water churned beneath the bow as it backed into the river and chugged upstream.

Because of the delay, leader Boyd Walker diverted our team to two unreached villages on the bank of a large lake, accessible only when the Amazon was high. The Amazon was at the highest water level in recorded history that year.

International travel required several inoculations, including yellow fever and tetanus, and we took malaria preventative medication. By the time we arrived in Manaus, I was racked by severe bone and joint pain because of the tetanus vaccine, which plagued me throughout the trip.

On the third night, moving slowly upstream with painful joints, I realized I slept among six men, one of whom was Donnie. For some reason that struck me as funny. Mama would have been mortified to hear me tell this part of the story. The inner giggling about my odd situation eased the pain of the tetanus reaction and the frustration of being delayed, fulfilling the proverb, "laughter does good like a medicine."

The fresh water was so high, it seemed as if we floated in an ocean. A definite line could be seen where the freshwater entered the Atlantic and the salt water began. In a living *National Geographic* moment, I realized the line between salt and fresh could be seen precisely and it did not mix, a confirmation that our Creator set boundaries in His creation, measured the earth with a span and confined the water within His designated firmaments.

One night, one of our boat mates asked if we wanted to go hunt alligators. I did not want to hunt an alligator, but I did want to see the stars in the Southern Hemisphere without light pollution. So, Donnie and I struggled into the small canoe-type boat and floated into the night with a guide and hunter. As we muddled along on the river and the guide shined a light into the vegetation along the bank to see if bright eyes could be noticed, I kept my eyes on the sky in hopes of seeing stars in the southern hemisphere. I kept asking the Lord to remove the haze that clouded my view, so I had a clear view of the stars.

Suddenly, I realized I wasn't looking at a fog or haze, but the Milky Way, millions upon millions of stars so dense it appeared as a shroud hovering between the earth and the universe. Marvelous! Beautiful! Amazing! As I rejoiced in my heart for being among the vastness of His earth, Donnie said, "There is the Southern Cross!" Sure enough, the eye candy became even sweeter.

We brought back the small alligator caught during our excursion to the large boat. We petted it and took photos of it then we let it go. The boat cook offered us alligator meat on board. I declined.

After a good night's sleep in hammocks and a hearty breakfast, we continued along the swollen Amazon. As our group neared the lake area of our village destinations, we saw pink dolphins jumping alongside the boat. I did not know these existed. Another in-person *National Geographic* moment presented itself.

A smaller craft went ahead of the larger boat to make sure the water was high enough to get from the river into the lake area, and to cut away any vegetation that might clog the motor on the larger craft. With the all clear, our group went out into the lake area to the first of two villages, Sao Paolo and Sao Pedro, a.k.a. St. Paul and St. Peter. Sao Pedro used fresh running water from faucets in a trough to serve the population. Our guide made arrangements to come back by Sao Pedro in a few days to present a Bible school for the children, bring supplies, and host a dental clinic. We disembarked for a few hours, then rejoined the boat to go to Sao Paulo. We tied off and unloaded for a building project and Bible school.

Our team was a highly-skilled one. One man brought small flutes for the children to learn to play. A hairdresser gave hair cuts. A dentist pulled teeth. Due to the amount of tannic acid in the drinking water, people of Sao Paulo sometimes lost their permanent teeth by the time they reached adulthood. I assisted the dentist for two days. He pulled teeth to the tune of flutes coming through an open window where I could see the long line of Sao Paulo citizens lined up to get haircuts.

One lady coordinated Bible school for the children with several others who helped. Other men on the team, including Donnie, worked on building projects, like transforming a small porch into a small kitchen.

An EMT took blood pressures and offered basic wound care. One evening he traveled by canoe to an island in the lake where a woman was giving birth. Baby and mom were fine, he reported upon his return to Sao Paulo. The big smile said it all.

On our final evening in Sao Paulo, we shared a worship service and food. We drank bottled water because we could not drink the water. The village needed a well for fresh water. Upon our return to the United States, Grace Missionary Society received designated funds to drill a well for the village of Sao Paulo.

After three days, our team boarded again and returned to Sao Pedro. We held a Bible school, pulled teeth, and unloaded food for the locals.

While in Sao Paulo, I offered a boy of about ten, money for his wooden paddle. I was not sure how or if I could get it through the airport. However, I prayed the Lord would make a way. When we arrived at the airport, staff told me to take the paddle to an oversized luggage counter. Airport personnel wrapped it and shipped it on our plane. When we reached the States, Customs employees unwrapped and checked the paddle for insects before allowing it to enter the U.S. I was grateful to display it at New Beginnings for several years after our trip, a reminder that a delay is not God saying, "No," but, "Wait and see what I will do through my servants."

Mongolia

Having accepted an invitation to a tea in Stillwater, Oklahoma, I sat with strangers at a round table at the Oklahoma State University during a presentation hosted by the Assembly of God English as a Second Language program. A woman from Mongolia sitting across the round table from me introduced herself. During the meeting, Dawaa and I discussed our travels. I shared with her about Grace Missionary Society. As we left the meeting, she asked me to help the children of Mongolia. Without a second thought, I agreed to help. She gave me her sister's contact information in Mongolia.

I contacted her sister in Ulaanbaatar to ask what she needed to assist the children of Mongolia. After several virtual conversations, she introduced me to a young teacher in Mongolia who took the message of Jesus Christ to other teachers across the vast plains of Mongolia. Teachers trained teachers and in the process, shared the gospel with them. The teacher's group also met with other Christians to pray for Mongolia, sometimes spending up to a week in one city praying for their countrymen.

Grace Missionary Society has sent small offerings to this teacher's group to help them share the gospel through teaching teachers. Little is much in the hand of God through His people.

*****

China

George and Shirley, along with another couple from McLoud, traveled to China long before Grace Missionary Society formed. It seems George Palmer lived the Hank Snow ballad, "I've Been Everywhere." But I preferred to do all my China outreach in the prayer closet.

Many years after his trips to China, George invited me to meet a missionary he met in China who was coming to his house to stay overnight. The meeting lasted several hours, long enough for the Holy Spirit to slip in a little nugget putting the people of China at a higher level on my prayer radar. Since that visit, Grace Missionary Society shared designated offerings with the missionary and many prayers for the people of China.

*****

Grace Missionary Society also sponsored discipleship opportunities for youth and youth groups in several nations including the Ivory Coast, Macedonia, Ukraine, Norway, and Mali. A donation from Australia provided a pin prick touch to this continent.

*****

Personal traveling during which I prayed for countries were adventurous in different way. Time was enjoyed with family and friends, while also praying for every place upon which my feet stepped. I figured the promise of God to the children of Israel that their inheritance included where their feet stepped (Deuteronomy 11:24), also pertained to the One I advocated for in the earth. For each state or country or county or city, I claimed that the Spirit of God would invade these places to stir the hearts of people to call them to their Destinys.

As I enjoyed vacations with family and friends. It has been my joy to step on land in every state of the United States, except three, Connecticut, Rhode Island and Oregon. I hope to add these. In addition to those featured above, Donnie and I traveled to Canada, Mexico, Honduras, Belize, France, England, Wales, Ireland, Spain, Switzerland, The Netherlands, Germany, Italy. Our experiences in these places could fill books. Even though I did not become a great pianist, while in Donnie's family home in Mogelsberg, Switzerland, I played a pipe organ in the only church in town. While in France, I played "It is no Secret What God Can Do," on the Napoleon family piano. Donnie and I stepped onto the sands of Normandy where we honored Allied forces for their sacrifices for freedom. In The Netherlands, we toured the clock shop where the Ten Boom family sheltered Jews. Dachau concentration camp in Germany revealed what happened to most members of that family and millions more.

My journey was not walked alone. Those who went before me trod the same path. Many prayed the same prayers for their generations. I only added my voice to the millions who went ahead and prayed the same prayers and voiced the same praises in their generations. Modern transportation developed long before I was born, made my journey possible. Modern technological advances opened the path for me to build on the foundations others laid.

Chapter 27
Conclusion

"Even when I am old and gray, do not forsake me, O God, till I declare your power to the next generation, your might to all who are to come." Psalm 71:18 NIV

At seventy years old, I look back at my life and wonder how I arrived on top of a mountain overlooking the city of Sliven, Bulgaria, a city I did not know existed until I arrived there in 2000. I numbered the dreams and visions I had and considered the pathway of completion for each one.

A stream does not choose its path but follows an unseen gravitational flow. I did not choose the life I lived, but, our Creator knows the soil in which we can best grow.

There is no way to estimate the number of people touched through the life of another. Statistics of a day to day ordinary life are not often kept. My own journals focus more on the five senses of experience. The churches and organizations in which I served did not keep records of individual participation of the teams in which I played a small part.

Grace Missionary Society did not keep statistics about the number of lives changed, meals offered, children educated, or churches constructed. Like a flowing mountain stream, the Grace team ran too fast to count.

As I review it in my mind, I begin to understand the scripture in John about Jesus: the world could not hold the books that could be written about the things He did or the people He touched (John 21:25). The Kingdom of God is like a great network thrown into the sea gathering from all nations those who fear God. It is impossible to calculate. Some sow, others water, and many reap of the same harvest.

God allowed me to be part of His body of believers who shared my generation. I cannot boast. How could I? I did nothing but carry a willing heart. God allowed the circumstances to play out like a novel written from the eternities. I could not have comprehended this life. I read about my journey and sense I am writing about someone else's life, instead of a little girl who simply survived in small town Oklahoma.

I never received a financial benefit from the McLoud Historical Society Museum and Heritage Center or Grace Missionary Society. Joy in creating, contributing to that which could continue was my salary.

Whatever failure you notice in my journey, let it become a lesson well-learned. There is none truly good but God. Let my childhood speak to parents, and let my youth relate to those who stumble into unhealthy, uninformed decisions. When we humans are faithless, even then, God is faithful. Trust His promises. May my fears and insecurities be relatable. May any pain anyone incurred because of my decisions, be healed. May my unnoticed back-stitches hold firm in the quilt of life.

May the reading of my journey be fruitful. May it confirm the love of God through Jesus Christ our Lord.

My prayer for those who read my story is:

Whatever fruit-bearing seeds lie within you, let the wind of the Holy Spirit carry them around the earth where they continue to fall into good soil, produce and are planted again.

May the blackberries you produce be sweet.

Since no backstitches are allowed in this life, may your path be straight.

May death be overcome by life as you journey through this earth.

Glenda Palmer-Kuhn

May your life light the way your travels take you to another generation of faith-walkers and dream catchers.
Amen.

Meet the Author

Former newspaper publisher/editor Glenda Kuhn has penned many stories throughout her writing career. As President of McLoud Historical Society, she has contributed to three books for the McLoud Historical Society Museum and Heritage Center.

Now focusing on children's books, each of her books has a basic life lesson for beginning readers. The books also introduce children to social interaction. She lives in her hometown of McLoud, Oklahoma.

Glenda Palmer-Kuhn

Other Books By Glenda

Aliyah Likes Being A Giraffe

Delilah Dances One Step at a Time

Friend Philia

Let's Be Friends, A Jungle Legend

Mattie

Powerful Emajen-ation

Sir Locksalot Loses His Keys

Made in the USA
Middletown, DE
09 October 2022